Iron Mantis Martial Arts
Black Belt Manual

A guide for all Iron Mantis practitioners

Our Mission, Vision, and Goal.

Iron Mantis Mission Statement - To reduce human suffering by practicing martial arts. To preserve the Chiu Leun lineage of Seven Star Praying Mantis. To teach this style of Chinese Martial Arts to all regardless of gender, ethnicity or religion. To promote professional martial arts, fitness and health while keeping an open mind. This training will in turn discipline the mind, body and spirit, leading us to a happier, healthier and more harmonious existence.

Our *Vision* is to promote Iron Mantis Martial Arts to help as many people as possible live a mentally and physically healthier lifestyle.

Our *Goal* is to have successful Iron Mantis Academies throughout the U.S. and abroad. This means teaching with high ethics and moral values and having a safe environment to nurture both young and old. Iron Mantis Headquarters will point the way, leading by example and setting the standards. Our main goal is to further learn and teach the Iron Mantis System which is made of many programs: striking techniques (effective combinations), offense without bridging and bridging techniques, chi sau (no-mind training), jim lim sau (trapping hands), chin-na (joint-locks / seize and control), Jiu-Jitsu (grappling / takedowns and ground controlling), ditang (ground fighting), taijiquan, qigong, posting, yoga, strength and conditioning (sports performance training for competitors), traditional forms training along with classical and modern weapons.

Our Purpose and Intention

Purpose is the thing you want to achieve, especially something that you are determined to do or get.

Intention is the idea or plan of what you are going to do. Stay on Purpose and harness the Power of Intention.

The Iron Mantis Association will assist other sifus, instructors, and school owners to implement Iron Mantis programs into their system. The Iron Mantis Association will offer affiliate instructors a way to earn a living while helping spread Iron Mantis Martial Arts throughout their community and the world. We offer consulting, camps, and retreats in order to learn, train and share new ideas, all while bringing our international family together. Affiliates can receive class planners, affiliate recognition with the IMMA name and logo, business and marketing ideas, day-to-day operations support, policies and procedures, and more hands-on training. Whether an affiliate, an associate, a family member, or a networking member, our goal is to be able to spend more time with one another, furthering our skills and enjoying each other's company. It's the love for martial arts that brings us together and the love for one another that makes us family. We train on the floor together!

We are constantly working on documentation of the system, videography, and publications. Black Belts must bring something to the table helping to improve the Association. We'll continue growing

and supporting our wellness network of doctors, acupuncturists, chiropractors and sports therapists, staying informed on diet and nutrition, herbs, supplements, training research and recovery methods. Sifus will write articles and publish, create videos and stay updated on the newest technology to help keep our systems up to date. Lastly, the Coaches will help the Iron Mantis Association wherever they can, however they can - they will find a job and fill it. Coaches will assist Sifus in teaching and educating the public, but most importantly by continuing to train diligently, moving forward in both skills and knowledge. In general, Coaches develop Black Belts, Sifus guide the Coaches, and Masters further develop sifus. Iron Mantis is a complete martial arts system which encompasses health, self-defense, competition and overall well-being. I recommend working your forms daily, developing your Sadhanna and getting a good night's rest.

There are no shortcuts to mastery (comprehensive knowledge or skill in a subject); hard work and time spent in martial arts is a must to build your craft. True masters are rare and a gift to society. To practice martial arts is to cultivate one's opponent and harmonize with one's surroundings. Practice first for health, second for defense. There are no secrets, just knowledge, the master points the way and you must do the work. If you know how to train you'll always improve, if not you can train for two lifetimes and achieve nothing.

"Practice diligently and the truth will unfold itself"

功夫

Our Grandmaster Chiu Leun in New York City

Foreword

Life is a wonderful funny thing for those individuals that are alert to its wonders. And on one such occasion it brought my brother Jeff for me to meet. Now sometimes you meet people that you never see again and some you continue to build lasting bonds with. Jeff has been the kind that I have built a lasting bond with from the very start of our introduction together. His sincere humbleness and desire to learn coupled with his willingness to freely share knowledge was apparent from the start and has continued ever on. The iron mantis system is the ultimate culmination of many years of hard work and painstaking perseverance crafted in the fires of pain. For those

功夫

that have chosen the martial path as their way of life I can say this wholeheartedly, there is no better way than the iron mantis system for developing fully rounded martial artists (not ruffians) who know what respect, honor and humbleness means plus what being part of a true martial family means.

Much luck and prosperity on your martial journey.

- Sifu Louie Ginorio

I met Jeff at a USA national martial tournament in the 1990s. We were competing in the same straight sword division. He got first place, and rightly so. I got maybe fourth place. My firm was boring and poorly done. The thing was that one of his people was keeping scores for everyone and noted I was scored incorrectly and noticed my score should have been higher. Jeff was informed, and he actually told the judges, and my score was changed, and I think I got third place. Afterward, I thanked Jeff and his friend for their respect and honesty. At that point, we realized his teacher was my senior Gung fu brother Raymond Fogg. After that, we became good friends and shared information, off and on, and have tried to make strong connections between various martial groups and individuals.

Jeff Hughes Book is an honest and sincere attempt to present particular Chinese martial traditional ideas, elements of basic classical Chinese history, and contemporary concepts of certain combat methods. Jeff particularly addresses some of the historical background of the Sifu Chiu Leun, from Hong Kong,

功夫

and his Sect of 7 Star Mantis in New York. Much of this history is not widely known and even disputed by some. He presents the topic in a respectful manner and uses valid sources. Jeff Hughes endeavors to make a bridge on one side with various contemporary ideas in culture, sport science and the general current public interest in physical arts and on the other side his past experiences and ideas he has been exposed to from years of practice. He truly uses the "art" part of martial arts and shows his creativity while trying to respect the elements that make up Iron Mantis. His book is appropriate for those beginning and intermediate practitioners of martial arts and fitness interested in improving their depth of knowledge of the dimensions of 7 Star Manis and aspects of the bridge between Chinese, Buddhist, and Yoga of India. - Sifu Nathan Chukueke

功 夫

Table of Contents

功夫

功夫

An Introduction to Iron Mantis

I'm writing this book as an outline for my students and as an introduction to new readers. A close friend and martial arts brother passed away too early in life and I told myself I would document everything I know to teach my students and for future prosperity. I remember his plan was to create a manual with a clear curriculum, theories, concepts and principles to pass onto his students and instructors. When he passed he had not been able to finish his life goal and left many of his students without a clear manual. I promised myself in his honor to document all my teachings, all the lessons taught to me, all the knowledge I've accumulated. For my students I have this book and videos

功夫

that correspond with each other. For those new to Iron Mantis Martial Arts I hope to show my life's work and inspire other teachers and students to do the same. I hope this book can somehow motivate any practitioner to make it a pursuit to study martial arts as a way of life and as a way to give back to society. Whether for a student or a teacher of any discipline I hope this book can offer some type of assistance, guidance or motivation. I love all martial arts and I feel we are one family, we are more similar than different. Respect to all the masters before us.

   - In memory of my brother Richard Feagin

Autobiography of Sifu Jeff Hughes

To better understand the beginnings of Iron Mantis Martial Arts it helps to understand my history of martial arts and exposure to violence. I always lived in rough areas growing up and the times were much different. As a result, I began training in Kajukenbo in 1974, a Hawiian style of martial arts known for its proven modern street effectiveness. Shortly after I began training, I was able to defeat my first school yard bully. From Kajukenbo I went on to study a number of different Korean styles of martial arts. Since I moved around a lot as a kid, I was unable to reach my black belt in these styles. I would settle into a new area, start making friends, begin training in another amazing art, and then I would have to move again. This gypsy nomadic lifestyle brought with it many lessons, and the pros and cons eventually all turned into pros.

功夫

I was born in Oakland, California in 1967, living in Concord, Vacaville and Pittsburg, CA through the 70's and 90's, and in between, in the 80's, in Seattle, Washington and small-town East Texas. Everywhere I lived I honed my martial skills as best I could, and from city to city and state to state I had many opportunities to apply what I had learned in my martial arts classes.

In the early 80's I started training Hapkido and Kuk Sul Won in East Texas aka "Behind the Pine Curtain." East Texas in the 80's was a training ground unto itself as fighting was a daily occurance, a way of life. I was never the tough guy as I was surrounded by natural born savages. Respect was earned and character was developed. Hapkido was brutal and I loved it. Classes generally started off with lots of fitness - if you were soft coming in you left hardened in no time. After fitness was mitt and bag work, drilling techniques and quickly moving to sparring. We sparred every class and beatings were regular, as it should be, for this is what prepared us for the real world. It was tough love, no talking in class and bringing your "A" game each class. Each belt test the sensei lined up the whole school and you sparred every student from lowest to the highest rank. Tests were designed to break you down and make you fail. You got to the point where you wanted to quit, but you didn't; you pushed through and earned your place in the dojo. When you get beat-up enough you're fine with dishing it back out, that's how we sharpened each other.

Almost all of my martial arts teachers had been in the military and had served in Vietnam. Most of my teachers were Marines which brought a mindset and discipline to the training that I

功夫   3

loved. It was important that our training worked in a real fight.
In those days students did not join a martial arts school to meet
new people or create community - we joined to learn how to
fight. No matter the style, when you came across a black belt
they were to be respected.

In January 1992 I began my training with Sifu Raymond Fogg,
an 8th generation master of Seven Star Praying Mantis Kung Fu.
Sifu Fogg was also a black belt in Taekwondo and Judo and had
served as a marine in Vietnam. He was originally from
Washington, D.C. and had trained in New York City's
Chinatown furthering his Praying Mantis Kung Fu studies.
Together Sifu Fogg and I trained with Ho Yin Chung (student of
Won Han Fan) and his son Henry Chung. I went on to become a
Sifu under Master Raymond Fogg. I also trained in NYC in
most of the boroughs. In 1997 I went to Hong Kong to meet and
train with Seven Star Mantis Grandmaster Lee Kam Wing. I
went on to train with all the elders in our lineage, from Carl
Albright, Stephen Laurette, Nathan Chukueke, Chiyu Ho,
Stanley Moy, Tony Puyot then finally with Sifu Raymond
Nelson and his student Louie Ginorio. I have been training
under Raymond Nelson since around 2005. My Sifu Raymond
Nelson is the head of the Iron Mantis Clan. Our late
Grandmaster Chiu Leun learned from the Yip Ming Duk Jee
Monks and Chiu Chi Man and often returned to visit and train at
their Buddhist Temple in China in the New Territories.

功夫

The Abbot with Chiu Leun

I have trained other styles of Kung Fu, such as the Southern Hung Gar aka Tiger Crane System under Josephus Clovin, or Kung Fu Joe, whose nickname was given to him by the Karate guys on the East Coast. Sifu Colvin would go into schools and challenge their Senseis, and whoever lost would give up their black belt which was a common thing back in the day. Similarly, if there was a phony school and teacher in the community, someone would go there, beat them up and close the school. I also studied Eagle Claw Kung Fu with Grandmaster Lily Lau, daughter of the late Grandmaster General Lau Fat Man. I trained extensively in Yang Family Taijiquan with Sifu Horacio Lopez and the Yang family. Also with Sifu Lopez, I

功夫

5

studied a little Beijing Wu Taijiquan, an amazing system and lineage of scholars and fighters under Wang Peisheng.

Through the years I have had many accomplishments in martial arts competitions as well as fight clubs. I competed strictly in Karate tournaments throughout the 80's, fighting as much as possible. In the early 90's, looking for a change I started attending the USA Wushu Kung Fu Federation Regional, National and International Tournaments, going on to become an International Champion in both forms and fighting. In the summer of 2000 I traveled to China and Hong Kong with Grandmasters Lily Lau and Brendan Lai for additional training and to compete in the Qingdao and Beijing International Martial Arts Tournaments. I won a silver medal at the International Wushu Championship in Qingdao and a silver and bronze in Beijing. Jet Li's teacher Wu Bin ran the Beijing Tournament, and it was a special time on many levels. I became a judge in many different tournaments and an official for the AAU Chinese Martial Arts Division. After competing in Chinese martial arts tournaments for 10 years, I went on to run tournaments for nearly a decade.

In time, service to others and creating a positive impact in people's lives became a larger focus of my martial development. As a result, from 1995-2005 I was constantly doing charity for the Austin School district, Austin Children's Museum, St. Judes Children's Research Hospital, the Austin Public Libraries, and Austin Juvenile Detention Center to name a few. I went on to form the "Friends of Peace," a meditation awareness movement in Austin, TX. I also highly promoted the healing practices of Qigong, Tai Chi (taijiquan) and Yoga.

功夫

The increasing importance of improving lives motivated and propelled what became a highly successful martial arts school in South Austin, Texas for over 20 years. It began as a traditional Kung Fu school and grew into a modern MMA and fitness facility known as The Pit Austin. After running the school for several years, I decided to further my education and earned a black belt in Hawaiian Kempo (and a CrossPit coach certification) under Grandmaster John Hacklman and a black belt in KORE Brazilian Jiu-Jitsu under Professor Luigi Mondelli of American Top Team. From there I became a USA Weightlifting Advanced Coach and trained olympic lifting and sports performance under Lance Hooton, SCCC and USA Weightlifting Senior Coach. After realizing I needed more Wrestling skills for myself and my school's programs, I trained with Kenny Johnson of BOLT Wrestling who wrestled under legendary Dan Gable and trained for 7 Olympic Games. Finally, I trained Iyengar Yoga under Bekir Algan, my teacher and good friend, and underwent his teacher training. From 1997 to 2017 I trained yoga under Bekir. Times are always changing, from the 70's, 80's and 90's into the 2000's the age of the internet, social media and all the modalities of learning, we are doing our best to help our communities and society by sharing the knowledge of health and wellness with martial arts. In sum, I'm always learning; I keep the "Beginner's Mind" and I strive to always be moving forward—no matter how that looks or feels.

Sifu Chiu Leun in his Kwoon, New York City

The Origins of Iron Mantis

Iron Mantis Martial Arts is a complete martial arts system created by Sifu Jeff Hughes, culminating from years of training and experience. It is mainly three martial arts systems combined into one. Seven Star Praying Mantis Kung Fu (Traditional), Hawaiian Kempo (MMA) and Brazilian Jiu-Jitsu (BJJ) are the main components of the system. Iron Mantis combines these martial art styles into one system, combining styles in a way that works seamlessly, and was 20 years in the making. Respect to all the masters that came before us.

功夫

Iron Mantis Martial Arts, or Iron Mantis for short, is a white through black belt program then 1st degree through 10th degree system with international standards. I have included Sports Performance Training (USAW and CrossPit) aka Iron Mantis Strength and Conditioning. It also includes Taijiquan, Qigong and Yoga. Diet and nutrition is essential to working up the belt ranks in a healthy, balanced way. Iron Mantis martial artists are essentially power-speed athletes. Iron Mantis has produced full-contact kickboxing, MMA, and BJJ champions as well as champions in forms and weapons competition. Besides that, we have worked with and further developed many amazing human beings - beautiful people who have in turn bettered our communities. There are many ways to measure if a martial art "works," first is always its effectiveness in self-defense and competitively, then improving health mentally and physically by strengthening the body and by benefiting those of all ages.

功夫

Sifu Chiu Leun in Hong Kong

功夫

Roots of Iron Mantis

Ancient masters practiced Kung Fu not just for self-defense, but as a way to benefit themselves on a physical, mental and spiritual level. Methods of competition vary throughout time and it's important to be relevant for the times. In times of hardship, such as the economic states faced before, this knowledge is imperative. Our Kung Fu helps us cope with our modern, fast-paced lives that can so often lead to stress, anxiety and illness.

The legend of the Shaolin Temple and its Shaolin Kung Fu monks began around 540 CE. The story goes that when an Indian monk Damo traveled to China to see the emperor and spread Buddhism. Damo introduced the Shaolin monks to the eighteen movements later to be known as 18 Lohan Qigong derived from traditional Indian Yoga. This was designed to increase their physical and mental strength as well as the flow of chi (life energy). It was these eighteen movements that would become Kung Fu as we know it today, after being perfected and expanded upon for nearly 2,000 years. I see no separation between Shaolin Kung Fu and Yoga. History is a way to pay respect as well as showing respect and sometimes an origin story. When we look at the story of Shaolin, we see the benefits that Kung Fu was originally intended to give us. The Shaolin monks began practicing Kung Fu not only for self-defense, but as a way to improve their health and spirituality. Kung Fu has been continually perfected over the centuries, creating the vast array of styles and variations that we know today.

The roots of the Iron Mantis Martial Arts system is Northern Shaolin Seven Star Praying Mantis martial arts, handed down from our late Grandmaster Chiu Leun. Kung Fu (pronounced Gung Fu) is a skill derived through hard work and time, and Wu Shu is the war arts. *Gung Fu Wu Shu* is the most correct term (a skill derived through hard work and time in the war arts). Although Kung Fu has changed over time and often becomes more focused on the "martial" side of things, the core message and philosophy remains the same as what Damo taught the Shaolin monks nearly 2,000 years ago, teaching exercises for health and meditation along with Buddhist sutras.

Bodhidharma, Damo or Daruma to the Japanese, was the 28th Indian patriarch and first patriarch of Zen Buddhism in China. He is believed to be of Brahman heritage and perhaps of royal blood. As an old man he undertook a mission to fulfill the wishes of his dying master to bring Buddhism to China. There are many legends of this sage, the Buddhism he taught at the Shaolin Temple eventually became known as Chan or Zen in its Japanese reading. The practice of meditation was the key to awakening one's inner nature, compassion and wisdom.

It is said that Damo remained facing a wall in a cave on top of the Shaolin Monastery for nine years before he began to teach. Damo quickly discovered that the Shaolin monks were in very poor physical condition and could not sit for the long meditation sessions demanded by his regimen. More than likely, drawing on the martial arts training Damo would have received as an Indian scholar, he devised exercises to develop strength, flexibility, balance and mental focus. Known as the Muscle Tendon Changing Classics, these became the foundation of

Shaolin conditioning, which developed into Shaolin Kung Fu. Damo is often regarded as the "Patron Saint" or the founder of Shaolin Kung Fu. Respect to the Shaolin Temple.

The Iron Mantis Mindset
Our way is in training 鐵 螂

From want comes grief - want what you already have. Iron Mantis basics are clearly defined, the answers are honest, the techniques are explained, the system is alive. Our *Righteous Harmonious Fist* guides us, Wu De (morals and ethics) will keep us humble. Hard work, time, patience, control, and understanding the Truth, which is always present on the floor, keeps us honest. So, without effort we lead by example. Our loyalty is in our actions not just in our words. We protect our mind like we protect our body.

Our way is in training; the master was once the beginner, is always a student, and understands sadhana (daily practice). Once you enter there's no turning back, the first step has been made, your words were heard and the path was set. During the Bai Si ceremony the disciple offers the tea, a toast to the beginner's mind. From Shaolin to the Iron Mantis Training Hall, the forms have carried the Keys.

Kuen - Chinese term for "form" aka *kata* is a tool for meditative and practical purposes, and is an encyclopedia of martial knowledge. The advanced forms in our Iron Mantis system make a difference in our development and skill level, they are not the same as lower and mid-level forms training. These advanced forms hold structure and knowledge that manifests on the floor while playing hands (freestyle sparring with no-gear). The full potential of these forms are most beneficial to the students who have mentally, physically and emotionally worked their way through the lower and mid levels of our system. There are no shortcuts, and those looking for them will not ascend to the higher levels. For beginners a form can be good exercise and something to talk about but to an advanced student the same form can offer much more, it can become a catalyst for the mind, body and spirit.

Our beyond black belt curriculum is more advanced techniques in all areas of combat, exercises to improve our health and our forms training. Many beginners start off understanding these forms simply as self-defense practices, in time you will discover that they are kinetic *"keys,"* to the elemental *"door"* to consciousness. This orientation towards understanding the mind is one of the reasons they were preserved and passed down through the masters in our lineage. Like Yoga, it's a practice that helps your body feel better and your mind to calm down by being in the moment. This feeling lingers after training, helping you find your center, a place where you are not overthinking. These practices help you stay calm, cool and collected.

The word *mandala* is a Sanskrit term that simply means "circle." A mandala can be defined in two ways: These can be seen externally as a schematic visual representation as in the shapes representing the chakras taught in *yoga*. And internally as a guide for several psychophysical practices that take place in Shaolin gung fu, including *Meditation, Taijiquan and Qigong.*

In this way, when learning Iron Mantis you must "know" your forms.

> *Forms are not forms. They are constructed in the manner of illusion by your own mind. – Damo*

The *Diamond Sutra* is known to be one of the world's oldest printed books. This sutra is revered in Shaolin Temple and is very important in our Northern Shaolin Seven Star Praying Mantis Gung Fu lineage. The diamond is a symbol of a clear mind and represents a type of wisdom that cuts and shatters illusions to get to ultimate reality. It's this type of mindset needed to train, improve and evolve in Iron Mantis Martial Arts.

Our goal is non-violence; with that being said, many know martial arts and few of them understand violence. There are ways to nullify situations, like paying attention to your surroundings, watching for signs, or gaining reconnaissance and intel, to name a few. Learn how to blend in; learn how to be unseen, and know when to instead be seen. Remember the event does not care about you, and nobody is coming to save you. In a self defense situation don't bring a knife to a gunfight, and don't rush to your death. Understand the ways of Bushido. When it's a hand-to-hand "fist fight" and you cannot get out of it, hit first and hit hard. Remember, one punch can end a fight, and a throw can be the finishing move. Self-defense situations are not games with rules and time limits, there is no referee or medical staff waiting to treat your wounds or save your life. Our goal is to knock out our opponent without being taken down. We only use trapping hands and wrestling if our strikes did not work, and we only grapple on the ground if our striking, trapping hands and

wrestling did not work. If you end up mounted you've made at least six mistakes, and now it's a dog fight for survival. Watch for knives and other potential weapons. Train for the worst and hope for the best.

The Iron Mantis Path

The first step is the most important step.
You stand at the beginning of a long, hard road, the likes of which you have never trod before.
Others will fall by your side unable to persist.
They will try to pull you back and down with them.
Do not give in.
They will invent ways of distracting you or deterring you and disturbing you with words.
All are false.

Only the dream in your heart will keep you going.
Courage and patience are your swords,
Use them well and wisely.

Learn the ways to preserve rather than destroy,
Avoid rather than check,
Check rather than hurt,
Hurt rather than maim,
And maim rather than kill,
For all life is precious, and even that of the meanest creature on earth cannot be replaced.

The Seven Progressions in Iron Mantis

Everything is earned, nothing is given. Respect is also earned, in the same way humility is developed, by playing hands and rolling daily on the floor. Whether Gi or No-Gi, whether standing or on the ground, the truth is on the floor. These progressions were taken from levels of Kung Fu training as taught to me by my teachers, some influence from gymnastics, Hawaiian Kempo belt ranking and Sports Performance Training proficiency. The Seven Progressions is a balance of what I was taught and my own ideas for ranking, titles, studies and goals.

1. Student (a new member of the school)
2. Todei (an accepted "in the door" student of the sifu)
3. Black belt (one who has mastered the IM basics)
4. Coach (a disciple, one who has mastered the IM fundamentals)
5. Sifu (a "closed door disciple" of the master)
6. Master (Diamond Cutter)
7. Grandmaster (The Abbott)

The meanings behind the Iron Mantis uniforms, belts and patches: *The enso patch is to be worn by all students over the Heart. The square patch is worn by a sifu over the Heart.*

It is a true honor to be a part of the Iron Mantis family and our long respected lineage. It's our responsibility to uphold this high standard of training. We stand on the shoulders of Giants.

The Iron Mantis Belts

It's a long road to earning an Iron Mantis black belt, one where respect is earned everyday and humility is developed on the floor. A black belt earns respect, not demands it. Within our association, belts and rank means a lot, but realize on the street they only cover two inches and you must cover the rest.

When a new student puts on the uniform and the sifu ties on the white belt for the first time the student officially becomes a martial artist of that school. A martial artist upholds the old ways of loyalty and respect, righteousness, harmony and Wu De (martial arts morals and ethics). It is the job of the teacher/sifu to teach these virtues to the students.

The colored belts represent the hard work and time put into moving forward and improving as a martial artist. Once a student successfully graduates the basic program, there is a Tea Ceremony acknowledging the student as a "todei" in the eyes of his Sifu. A todei is a student who is now "in the door" of the Iron Mantis Training Hall. During the Tea Ceremony, the Sifu officially accepts the student into the family by drinking cha (tea) served by the student. The offering of the tea is a gesture and a gift accepted in silence, the old way. The todei then receives a deeper understanding of the school patch and is taught the significance and meaning behind it. The patch is sewn on the left chest over the heart. The new todei understands that this heart patch signifies a reference to the Heart Sutra and our long lineage of masters, practitioners and disciples of over 400 years. From Northern Shaolin Seven Star Praying Mantis Kung Fu to

Iron Mantis Martial Arts, we are one and the same.

With hard work and time the todei successfully graduates out of the basic and fundamental training programs by entering what we call the "the void". This is done by earning the brown belt. The brown belt training is one year of daily practicing, reviewing and getting in the best shape of their life. From there the black belt test date is set by the Sifu.

A black belt signifies the mastery of the Iron Mantis basics (Levels 1 & 2). Along with earning the time-honored black belt, the student receives a black belt certificate by the Sifu, something that can never be taken away. The beyond black belt curriculum is the Mantis forms, Taijiquan, Qigong, Posting and higher level combative techniques. All combat skills like striking, grappling, trapping hands, and playing hands (which includes rolling) are maintained and further developed. For many, the journey of a black belt turns towards becoming a 1st degree certified Iron Mantis Coach. One journey ends and a new journey begins. After three years of being a black belt mastering the fundamentals (Levels 3 & 4) and developing new skills under their sifu, the black belt becomes an Iron Mantis Coach, a huge honor and responsibility. An Iron Mantis Coach is ranked 1st-3rd degree black belts. An Iron Mantis Sifu is ranked 4th-6th degree black belts. A sifu is awarded the second patch, and the significance and the hidden meanings of the square patch are shared. 7th-9th degree coral belts are worn by our systems master instructors.

The Gi represents the external, it's formal and used for the Combat training. The Shaolin uniform represents our roots from the Shaolin (Sil Lum) Temple and can be worn for training forms, classical weapons, Qigong, Yoga and Taijiquan.

In essence, a black belt is a white belt that never quit. A coach is a black belt that never quit. Becoming a sifu is a responsibility more than it is a privilege. A master is modest, humble and a force to be reckoned with. Respect to the Masters.

鐵 螂 Student Creed

As part of my martial arts studies,

I will strive to learn *Patience*

and *Self-Control*,

I will conduct myself with *Integrity*

and *Loyalty*,

I will *Respect* those around me,

I will show *Humility, Righteousness*

and *Kindness* in both word and deed.

I will strengthen my *Will, Endurance,*

Perseverance and *Courage*.

鐵 螂 12 Virtues

Patience
An ability or willingness to suppress restlessness, annoyance, anger, pain, or misfortune, without complaint, when confronted with delay. Being quiet, steady in perseverance, diligent. Even tempered care.

Self Control
Having control or restraint of oneself or one's actions, feelings, etc. Self control is synonymous with self-discipline, self-restraint, willpower and level-headedness.

Integrity
Adherence to moral and ethical principles; soundness of moral character; honesty. The state of being whole, entire, or undiminished. To preserve the integrity of the kwoon/dojo.

Loyalty
Faithfulness to commitments or obligations. Loyalty connotes a sentiment of devotion held for one's country, creed, family, friends, etc. Feeling of allegiance. The act of binding yourself (intellectually or emotionally) to a course of action.

Respect
Esteem for or a sense of worth or excellence of a person, a personal quality or ability, or something considered as a manifestation of a personal quality or ability. Willingness to show consideration or deference. A courteous expression (by

word or deed) of esteem or regard. Feeling of friendship.
Courteous regard for people's feelings.

Humility
Modest opinion or estimate of one's own importance, rank, etc.
Respect for other martial arts styles. The quality or condition of
being humble. A lack of false pride.

Righteousness
Righteous conduct. The quality or state of being just or rightful.
Morally upright; without guilt. In accordance with virtue or
morality. Adhering to moral principles (that which is right, just,
good and correct in behavior as a human being).

Kindness
A kind act or favor. Being friendly and forgiving. Showing
generosity, charity, sympathy, compassion and tenderness. The
quality of being warmhearted, considerate and humane.

Will
The faculty of conscious and especially of deliberate action; the
power of control the mind has over its own actions. The power
of choice one has over their actions. Wish, desire, purpose or
determination.

Endurance
The power of enduring or bearing pain and hardships. The
strength to continue despite fatigue, stress, or other adverse
conditions.

Perseverance
Steady persistence in adhering to a course of action, a belief, or a purpose; steadfastness.

Courage
The quality of spirit that enables a person to face difficulty, danger, pain, etc., without fear; bravery. Have the courage to act in accordance with one's beliefs, especially in spite of criticism.

The Iron Mantis Fighting Stance

In Iron Mantis Martial Arts the fighting stance is traditionally called *Hou Shi* (monkey position). Its emphasis is on mobility and security. Proper execution of Hou Shi will determine to a certain degree the effectiveness of your defense, offense and mobility. Good mobility is essential for success as it allows for movement to a position of advantage. Distance, timing, and rhythm are manipulated by your footwork. Footwork should always be alive, rooted, fluid and mobile. The weight distribution of Hou Shi is 50/50, or equal between feet, allowing the quickest motions forward, backward and to each side. The knees are bent to allow a lower center of gravity and make you a smaller target. The front foot is flat on the ground and is turned in 45 degrees, the knee staying over the toes. This causes the leg to be turned at an angle, preventing the enemy from attacking the knee by locking it out. Also, the knees are over the toes to ensure the weight is over the foot, creating a strong foundation, and the foot turned in 45 degrees with a bent knee protects the groin from a straight-on attack. Turning in the foot is a compromise between protection of the groin and forward mobility. The rear leg points directly at the enemy and is off-set a few inches wide; this is to allow access to the enemy without having to move the front leg out of the way. The rear leg is also bent; its weight is on the ball of the foot for better forward mobility.

The upper body is bladed about 30 degrees which allows you to use both arms effectively in offense and defense. If you are too bladed, it makes your back almost impossible to defend, and places your rear hand so far back which makes it difficult to use offensively. If you are too squared up, it makes the body a larger target and positions the arms in locations that makes zone-defense difficult. Being too squared forward also exposes the centerline to attack. There are many major targets on the centerline such as the eyes, nose, throat, solar plexus and groin. Controlling the centerline allows you to control the position, balance, and leverage of your opponent and their ability to attack. Instead, the body is slightly bladed with the hands held up at shoulder height and width and elbows dropped downward. The lead hand is as high as your head and the rear hand is around your cheek with your elbow protecting your liver.

Keep the head straight to maintain the field of vision and proper perspective. The shoulders are over the hips to maintain balance and mobility. The body must remain relaxed. It's important that the stance does not break down once footwork is added. Always maintain your balance with a solid stance when blocking, evading, and striking. With a strong stance it's harder for your opponent to take you down, and with strong footwork it's hard for your opponent to strike you. Hit but do not get hit; throw but do not get thrown.

Chiu Leun and Chi Chi Man, Hong Kong.

鐵 螂 Code of Ethics

1. Always honor one's family without expectation of receiving. Strive for family honor because it is a lifelong responsibility.

2. Honor your teacher or teachers. Give and sacrifice without the expectation of receiving, as it is a lifetime responsibility to your teacher, who gives you the gift of the art.

3. Treat your fellow students as a brother or sister. By giving and helping them to be better, you will strengthen yourself.

4. Senior students, be humble. Treat junior students as equals, thus enabling you to have the respect and position of a senior.

5. Junior students, be respectful to your seniors. Their treatment of you as an equal is a sign that they are starting to understand a deeper meaning of Kung Fu and are worthy of respect. This humbleness is to be respected.

6. Never consider yourself knowledgeable, regardless of time in training. We are on a staircase that is very long with no apparent end.

7. Recognize that everyone will have strengths greater than yours, regardless of their time in the art. Try to help them with their weaknesses and your weaknesses will be eventually strengthened.

8. Senior students are responsible to demonstrate the Kung Fu Codes of Ethics in and out of the Kwoon. This demonstrates the strength of your art and makes good practitioners and teachers.

9. Many times you may not agree with policies or actions, but it is your responsibility to stand behind your teacher and strive for better understanding as junior students do towards you. Remember, the next step may give you a better understanding. A student can ask the teacher, respectfully, for further explanation and clarification.

10. Remember, a teacher is human. They make mistakes and have human problems like anyone else. Realize that no one will be a perfect example. It is this kindness and understanding that

makes you strong for appreciating their humanness and their quest for betterment.

11. Be an example of courtesy, regardless of what step you are in Kung Fu. Courtesy in and out of the Kwoon is a sign of strength. By giving courtesy, you get courtesy and respect. This is the same as the golden rule: do to others as you would have them do to you.

12. Allow constructive criticism and suggestions by anyone. Others can catch something that is very true and helpful, if you are open. Remember that we are all equal humans and that thinking we know a lot, means we know little.

13. Never openly criticize your teacher. Hold your doubts or criticism to yourself and possibly your view will change later on the matter. Criticizing your teacher says you are his/her equal in knowledge and experience. This is considered very poor code and essentially you need another teacher (I would say to criticize your teacher disrespectfully is bad, but to criticize your teacher in a respectful manner is not bad and will lead to growth for the teacher and the student). As indicated earlier, teachers are human also and make mistakes.

14. When your teacher is speaking, listen carefully, and never cut off your teacher when he is speaking. This shows you do not value his/her words. If your teacher is speaking to you it is because he/she is sharing knowledge, feedback or camaraderie. Don't take that for granted. Respect is at the center of this guideline. Wait to be recognized, and then speak.

15. Self Respect. A way to show pride is to carry yourself earnestly, try your best even if it's not up to your expectations.

16. Sparring practice is a practice in containing one's ego. Approach this practice with a smile and from that place you will become better at it. Containment of one's ego is essential for developing a proper mind and spirit.

17. The showing of too much power in any joint lock exercise shows you have low-level ego containment. Use of technique with kindness and appreciation is a sign of strength. To intimidate others is a low level action.

18. Tenacity. It is your responsibility to do your best in all classes. Do not allow yourself to just follow or stand idle. Keep practicing, regardless of your grasp of, or ability of the technique. It is your responsibility not to complain of tiredness or your ability to do the practice. Keep your frustrations to yourself. Through diligent and hard practice comes mastery.

19. Cleanliness. Refined cleanliness means a refined mind. Clean clothes and body show by example the honor and ethics you hold.

20. Never ask for knowledge. Let your teacher decide when you are ready. To ask is a sign that you have mastered what has already been given to you. Remember any knowledge has a lifetime of perfecting. Working hard on what you have is the first sign that you are ready for more and deserve it. The key is to be at the level to ask the type of questions that will lead you to more knowledge. Your teacher will know by the question(s)

you are asking, if you are ready for the answer or more knowledge.

21. Always remember your teacher's birthday or any special holiday. Give them a gift of appreciation from your heart, no matter how small.

22. If you are far away from your teacher and you visit them or any other teacher, it is proper to bring them a small gift each time. This can be food for casual visits or presents suitable for more important visits. This is traditionally important.

23. If you have had a falling out with your teacher, but want to reestablish your connection, it is most important to bring a gift upon your first contact and to give your humble apology. A good teacher will forgive most things, but disloyalty is never forgiven in a traditional Kung Fu Kwoon. A student who does anything against his teacher is never to be trusted.

24. Anytime one is at the same table preparing to eat in the presence of their teacher, they must wait till the teacher takes the first drink or bite before they do. This is a show of respect and courtesy.

25. Let your Kung Fu speak for you. The way is in training.

The Six Guiding Principles

1. Be *Skilled* – movement should be varied, unexpected and flexible.

2. Be *Tactful* – knock down your enemy by use of his own force.

3. Be *Bold* – attack without hesitation whenever there is an opening.

4. Be *Quick* – one sees your fists, but not your blows.

5. Be *Fierce* – hit every vital point.

6. Be *Practical* – each and every movement serves the purpose of either attack or defense.

From the East to the West to Iron Mantis

The Legendary Wong Long, creator of the famous Northern Shaolin Seven-Star Praying Mantis system of Kung Fu, developed this system while spending his days at the Shaolin Temple. Taking the best techniques from seventeen other styles of the time, Master Wong developed one of the most effective fighting systems ever developed in China. Some of these techniques include the Long Fist of Tai Cho, Short Fist of Un Yian, Monkey Style of Sun Tan and the throwing strokes of Wai

Tek. These techniques combined with the movements used by the praying mantis insect gave birth to the Seven-Star Mantis system. The Northern Mantis system remained in the Shaolin Temple for several generations until a wandering Taoist monk by the name of Abbot Sheng Hsiao Tao Jen came to visit the sacred grounds. After mastering the Mantis Style, Tao Jen left the Temple to be the first person to take this style out of Shaolin and throughout China. Tao Jen handed the system over to Li San Chen who established a security service called the Pui Kuk. Li was revered in Northern China and was known to thieves as "Li the Lightning Fist."

No one ever defeated Master Li. When Li was much older he searched for a worthy student until he met Wang Yung Sheng, a national boxing champion. Before he taught Yung Sheng, Li challenged the young champion to a friendly match. Yung Sheng was unable to even touch the older master; Li simply seemed to vanish. Once Li touched Tung Sheng, Li was immovable. Yung Sheng went on to become the third successor of the Mantis System.

Master Sheng passed his teachings to Fan Yuk Tang. Fan weighed in at over 300 pounds and was known for his iron palm. He achieved widespread fame in China by accepting an open challenge from a Russian fighter in the early 1870s. Traveling to Siberia, Fan defeated the Russian champion along with several other challengers. Master Fan's disciple Low Kwan Yu earned the title of fifth successor of the system.

Sifu Low Kwan Yu

In 1919, learning of Master Lo's reputation as a fighter, the committee of the Shanghai Chin Woo Athletic Association, hoping to fill the position of chief instructor, sent a representative to Shantung to invite Lo to Shanghai. Master Lo accepted the position and trained many successful students. It was his respect for Huo Yuanjia that he took the position. His fighting techniques proved themselves again when one of his top students, Ma Ching Hsin took first place at a national competition of Chinese Boxing.

The next successor, Chiu Chi Man, was already an accomplished martial artist when he met master Lo. The late Grandmaster

Chiu Chi Man first joined the Hong Kong Chin Woo Association in 1924 where he studied Shaolin Tan Tui style for six years. He also trained in the Eagle Claw system and Tai Chi Chuan. When Master Lo was honored as one of the "Four Superlords"of the Chin Wu Association, Chiu Chi Man began to follow him. In 1930, Chiu Chi Man committed his studies to the Seven-Star Praying Mantis System.

Chiu Chi Man disseminated the Seven Star Praying Mantis system to Chiu Leun. Chiu Leun already had a background in Mantis style through his apprenticeship at a temple with the "Big Monk" and "Little Monk". Later, Chiu Leun spread the art to America when he relocated to New York's Chinatown. It was here that Raymond Nelson began his studies under Sifu Chiu Leun. Raymond Nelson is one of the few "closed door" disciples to come out of New York City. Raymond Nelson aka "Iron Fist Nelson", Franklin Saulters, Ghi Yu Ho aka the Happy Buddha, Carl Albright, Stephen Laurette, Nathan Chuekeke, Raymond Fogg, and a few others continued to pass on the teaching. These elders of our system brought me in and shared the knowledge handed down to them by their Sifu Chiu Leun.

The Seven-Star Praying Mantis style as taught through Grandmaster Chiu Leun, Sifu Raymond Nelson and Sifu Carl Albright is a complete fighting system with many empty hand, weapons and two-person sets. Iron palm and iron arm training constitute just part of the advanced instruction, along with the 18 Lohan Heigong set.

The Seven Star Mantis system has a rich history, which dates back almost 400 years. The fifth successor, Master Low Kwan

Yu, became most famous after he was asked to teach at the Jing Mo (Chin Wu) Martial Arts Association, founded by Master *Huo Yuanjia*. Master Lo went on to become one of the Four Super Lords of the Jing Mo. He brought his teachings to Hong Kong from Shandong Province, China. From there he handed his teachings over to Master Chiu Chi Man who in turn handed his teachings to Master Chiu Leun.

Low Kwan Yu with family

The Iron Mantis Family Titles

Master / 師父
Sifu / Shifu
Teacher / Father

Teacher / 老師
Luosi / Laoshi
Old Teacher

Coach / 教練
Gaaulin / Jiaolian
Teach / Practice

Master's wife / 師母
Simou / Shimu
Teacher / Mother

Master's Master / 師公
Sigung / Shigong
Teacher / Grandfather

Founder / 師祖
Sijo / Shizu
Teacher / Ancestor

Master's Elder Brother / 師伯
Sibaak / Shibo
Teacher / Elder-uncle

Master's Junior Brother / 師叔
Sisuk / Shishu
Teacher / Junior-uncle

Master's Sister / 師姑
Sigu / Shigu
Teacher / Aunt

Eldest Brother / 大哥
Dai Sihing / Dage
Big Elder-brother

Elder Brother / 師兄
Sihing / Shixiong
Teacher / Elder-brother

Elder Sister / 師姐
Sije / Shijie
Teacher / Elder-sister

Junior Brother / 師弟
Sidai / Shidi
Teacher / Junior-brother

Junior Sister / 師妹
Simui / Shimei
Teacher / Junior-sister

Chiu Leun and Lee Kam Wing sitting with Chiu Chi Man

Traditional Ways of Iron Mantis

In the Chinese culture, a red envelope, red packet or red pocket in Kung Fu circles is called LiSee, (simplified Chinese 红包; traditional Chinese 紅包; pinyin *hóngbāo*; Peh-or-hi: *Âng-pau*) which is a monetary gift given during holidays or for special occasions such as a wedding, a graduation or the birth of a baby.

In Iron Mantis Martial Arts, LiSee is a polite way to offer money to your Sifu or another Sifu as a gift. Note, some clans refer to LiSee as HongBau. A Sifu teaches you skills and in return the student offers LiSee. It's up to the Sifu to accept the gift or not. Show respect when giving or receiving LiSee by handing and receiving with both hands. A gentle rooted stance and with eye contact and a respectful humble bow. We don't get on our knees. When buying things from your Sifu like books, classical weapons, Dit Da Jow, etc. the red envelope is not needed. Know the difference.

Although the red envelope was popularized by Chinese traditions, other cultures also share similar traditional customs.

The color red has an important meaning in Chinese culture. Red symbolizes fire, which has the power to drive bad luck away.

Money is often given to young kids by their parents, grandparents, relatives and friends to offer luck at the New Year. The amount of money given follows cultural superstitions. For example, the amount needs to be lucky and also an even number to reflect a happy occasion. Lucky numbers in Gung Fu Wu Shu are 18, 36, 108 etc. Be creative.

Odd amounts are typically given during sad occasions like funerals. The amount given should never contain the number four, which in Chinese means death.

Thus, unlucky numbers include 4, 44 or 444 and are bad luck, evil serpent shi shi shi. Fours are simply a bad number. Many don't like a room numbered 13. Similarly, many won't go in a room numbered 444.

It's good luck to give the Lion LiSee at Lion Dancing during special occasions. Lion dancing during Chinese New Year, grand opening of schools, and other auspicious occasions are also known to be lucky to those in attendance bearing witness.

Wrapping a gift with a red bow means it is from the heart, and it should not be given back. When accepting a business card use two hands and never put it directly in your back pocket, it deserves better attention than that. Be mindful of things, be considerate and polite in words and deeds.

It's all about respect, knowing your environment and staying humble. Actions speak louder than words. Respect and courtesy will open many more doors than force, a kind hand receives. When we bow one hand is closed and the other is open. Only speak when improving upon silence.

Our Northern Shaolin 7-Star Praying Mantis Lineage

Hung Fa Yi Bai Si - Discipleship

When an individual chooses and joins a martial arts school, there instantly begins a Sifu-student relationship with the Master of the school. You are considered one of the regular students and nothing is asked of you, nothing is demanded of you, as you are just there to learn Kung Fu. This individual typically sees the martial arts school as a hobby and as such their attendance may be sporadic. As a result, the progression of the individual may also be sporadic and unpredictable.

The longer a student trains the more likely they will no longer identify their Kung Fu training as just a hobby. That individual now wants to get a deeper understanding of the system. To some this may mean going from Basic Training into Fundamental Training and completing the "Todei" Tea Ceremony, where the student offers the teacher tea and makes the commitment to Black Belt.

Then, from Black Belt Training they enter the instructors program. Here they can obtain a certification as a Coach to teach the art and potentially make a profession out of Kung Fu and being a professional martial artist. There is another level of student who truly identifies with the system and wishes to make a lifetime commitment to the system and the family. Bai Si, also known as discipleship, is the next step the individual would take to be accepted into the Kung Fu family.

The term "Bai Si" should not be taken lightly. The traditional Bai Si ceremony may last for many days filled with activities ranging from taking oaths, tea (offering) ceremony, and much celebration. The tea offering, in the traditional sense, dictates whether the individual is being accepted in the Kung Fu family or not. The tea, offered to the candidate, may be spiced, very hot, or very cold. Consumption of the tea (offered by the Master of the system) without hesitation symbolizes one's loyalty and their promise to preserve the knowledge of the Kung Fu family and the system. Consumption of the tea by the Master symbolizes the acceptance of the candidate into the Kung Fu family. Each Sifu has their own way; some are not into big ceremonies and keep it simple.

After being accepted into the Kung Fu family, one is thought to be closer to the Master of the system than his/her own family/siblings. You are now in the eye of the system. Anything you do and don't do will have a very important meaning, not only to the school, but to the Master and the system. Bai Si, as in Eastern thinking, is thought of as the actual time when you start to learn Kung Fu. Beforehand, there may be corrections here and there, but now, you get an in-depth understanding of the system. As the training continues, the proper etiquette is to not ask for more material. The Sifu will know your progression and your period of advancement.

Bai Si, as explained, is a very important step and part of the Kung Fu family. Oaths, pledges, and promises are repeated and upheld by the individual throughout the course of the individual's standing in the family. With the proper guidance from the Master of the system, the disciples will carry on the system to the following generations.

The Kung Fu Family grows stronger together.

Our Iron Mantis lineage comes from the Yip Ming Duk Monks, Chiu Chi Man and Sifu Chiu Leun. Our Northern Shaolin Seven Star Praying Mantis system of Gung Fu was handed down to the disciples of Chiu Leun. From Raymond Nelson down to Louie Ginorio and Jeff Hughes and down to the next generation of students. Respect to all the masters who have kept this lineage alive, the future of Iron Mantis Martial Arts looks bright, long live the mantis!

Sifu Chiu Leun and the Yip Ming Duk Monks

On May 10th 1931, *Sifu Chiu Leun* (Pronounced Jew Loon) was born in the neighborhood of Luhng Pihng, in Lane Number Five,

Fau Sek Village, Toi Saan Country. Toi Saan is part of Gwang Dung Province not far from Hong Kong, and it is where the vast majority of Chinese people who immigrated to the U.S. before the 70's originated. Chiu Leun's father immigrated to the U.S. and became an American citizen, but later returned to Toi Saan to find a wife. Since Chiu Leun's father was an American citizen, Chiu Leun was able to gain his American citizenship as well, and he traveled back and forth between China and the U.S. throughout his life.

In 1937, when Chiu Leun was six years old, he was playing in the fields as usual when he saw a baby bird hopping around, learning to fly. Its movements attracted him and he followed the bird into the woods. There he met two other children about his own age, a boy and a girl, and began playing with them. After some time the two children's uncle, an older man and Buddhist monk, joined them. When the young Chiu Leun wanted to go home he was unable to find his way, and so the monk helped him get home.

The monk, boy and girl were from Northern China. The rest of the children's family had been killed, and so they and the monk, who was their father's brother, escaped to the south. Since then, the three had been living in the woods, collecting and selling medicinal herbs to support themselves. They also practiced Chinese Gung Fu. The monk was training to be able to return to the north and fight those who had killed his family.

A day or two after the monk helped Chui Leun find his way home, the monk returned to Chiu Leun's home and talked to his mother, saying that her son had a kind of affinity, a sort of uncanny connection with him and his niece and nephew. If she accepted the idea, Chiu Leun, her son, would leave home and go to live with the monk and two children. China in the 1930's was a fairly lawless and dangerous place. The Japanese occupied much of the north and were pushing south to extend their control. Ports were closed, and it was impossible for all but the richest and the luckiest to leave. Getting money in and out of China, or from America, was nearly impossible. So, the opportunity for a small child to go into apprenticeship tutelage with a monk was not to be dismissed lightly.

After returning twice to Chiu Leun's home, his mother agreed to allow the monk to take her son into apprenticeship. One of Chiu Leun's jobs would be to help as an interpreter and guide the northerners as they went. In exchange, he would learn the science of Chinese medicine, particularly what is called "Diht Da," treating injuries to the bones, ligaments, tendons and muscles. This training went along with learning Tohng Lohng Kuhyn (The Praying Mantis style of Chinese martial arts).

The four travelers lived in the woods, collecting herbs and selling them and other liniments and medicinal preparations across Guangdong and the surrounding areas. All the while Chiu Leun was learning more Gung Fu and how to fight with his hands and traditional weapons. He traveled and trained with the monk, his older gung fu brother, and his younger gung fu sister for ten years, until about 1947. The Japanese occupation was then over, but there was civil war in China between the Nationalists and the Communist armies. While the older monk resolved to return to the north to take revenge for his brother's family, he told Chiu Leun and his gung fu brother and sister, who now knew Tohng Lohng Kyuhn very well, to go to Hong Kong and find their younger gung fu uncle. Soon after, Chiu Leun discovered that both the monk and the enemy that had killed the monk's family both died in their fight.

Once in Hong Kong, it took awhile for Chiu Leun and the others to find their gung fu uncle. Chiu Chi Man was a gung fu sifu and taught Northern Eagle Claw (Ying Jaau Faan Ji Muhn), Mh Ga (Wu Style) Taai Gihk Kyunh (Tai Ji Quan), as well as Chat Sing Tohng Lohng at the Hong Kong Jing Mou Association. The Jing Mou had invited Lo Kwon Yu to come from Shanghai many years earlier to teach. Interestingly, Chiu Chi Man had learned a great deal of the same system that Chiu Leun had spent over two thirds of his young life studying and perfecting.

Sifu Chiu Leun once told a story about attacking his uncle and being thrown and hurt severely because the older man did not know it was his nephew who was playing around. Chiu Leun studied with Chiu Chi Man for about five years and always spoke of him with the greatest regard and respect. During this time Chiu Leun helped his uncle in the Jing Mo Association. The association occupied the sixth floor of a building and on the lower floor in the building opposite, there was another martial arts school. The school was owned by Bahk Mou Chiu ("White Haired" Chiu) the famous master of Hung Fat Pai. Chiu Leun took to watching the classes and, over time, picked up the entire Hung Fat Style. Later, he invited Sifu Bahk Mou Chiu out and, to show his respect and admiration, demonstrated what he had picked up, respectfully requesting corrections in his performance. Chiu Leun's understanding of Chinese Gung Fu was deep and broad; even this very different style had a few mysteries.

Throughout his time in Hong Kong, Chiu Leun kept in contact with his older gung fu brother and young gung fu sister. After he had been with his uncle Chiu Chi Man for five years or so, his gung fu sister decided to enter a Buddhist convent. Since his gung fu sister, whom he had known virtually his entire life had turned her back to the world, Chiu Leun located his younger gung fu uncle–the one his sifu had told him to look for in Hong Kong. Chiu Leun entered a temple with the younger gung fu uncle as well, where he studied several years, practicing Tohng Lohng Kyuhn from about 1952 to around 1957. After leaving convent in 1957, Chiu Leun reentered society and traveled around, making a living with the Chinese Herbology he knew well and practicing Chinese gung fu, both to attract clients and to protect himself. At this time much of rural China was "untamed."

Then, in 1966, Sifu Chiu Leun immigrated to New York. During the first year or so, he worked as a sort of security guard. Soon, he opened the first Kung Fu School in New York City's Little Italy, on Elizabeth between Broome and Grand Streets. In those days, Chinatown was much smaller and there were very few Chinese businesses above Canal Street. After a year, he moved one block away to 166 Mott Street, where he taught until 1984. After that, he taught only closed door disciples. Sifu Chiu Leun also founded the Eastern-America Martial Arts Association, but after some time decided to leave it to others to manage as they saw fit.

Chiu Leun and Raymond Nelson with students

For his entire professional teaching life, Sifu Chiu Leun never advertised for students. His reputation as an extraordinary practitioner of Chinese martial arts, in particular Chat Sing Tonhng Lohng Kyuhn, has never been and unfortunately is never likely to be equaled. On Sunday January 15, 2006, at 3:30 pm Sifu Chiu Cheung Leun passed to his next life in Beth Israel Hospital in New York City. He was survived by his two sons, Hing-Wah and Sing-Wah and two daughters, Siu-Bun and Man-Nei. He is sorely missed by all of his numerous students. We all wish him a pleasant life to come.

   - Sifu Stephen Laurette

Iron Mantis Black Belt Curriculum
An outline from white to black belt

Upholding Tradition for Modern Times

Iron Mantis Martial Arts
White to Blue Belt Curriculum
1st Chamber, 3 months of training

Bow: attention, set and salute.

Ebay (means begin). Sow (means end).

Bai Fut Sau (Buddha Palm Breathing) in horse-forward-crane.

Basic strikes: (fight stance), jab, cross, jab-cross, L hook, 1-2-3-bob & weave L & R. Shadow box, heavy bag, mitts, fit-sparring.

Basic stretch: (see stretch requirements).

Basic kicks: rising and snap (fight stance or forward stance).

Mantis Boxing: focus theory, 3-pattern block long-range.

Grapple (Jiu-Jitsu): side headlock defense, swim drill.
Solo drills: sprawl, backdrop, technical get-up,
buck and bridge, shrimp, hip heist, rolls.

Gong: (done everyday), horse stance B.F.S. 5 min.

Basic fitness: (see fitness requirements).

Iron Mantis Martial Arts
White to Blue Belt Curriculum
2nd Chamber, 3 months of training

Bow: attention, set and salute.
Ebay (means begin). Sow (means end).
Basic strikes: (fight stance), 4 punches and sprawl,
L hook-cross, 1-2-R front kick. Shadow box, heavy bag, mitts,
fit-sparring.

Basic footwork set: (solo and with a partner)
shuffle forward, back, inside, outside, circle.
(mirror drill w/ partner, cooperative and random).

Basic stretch: (see stretch requirements)
Basic kicks: inside crescent and outside crescent.
(fight stance or forward stance).

Fundamental form: 12 basic stances.

Mantis boxing: 3 pattern block mid-range.

Grapple (Jiu-Jitsu): over the knee takedown, mount escapes,
attacks from the top and bottom.
Solo drills: sprawl, backdrop, technical get-up,
buck and bridge, shrimp, hip heist, rolls.

Gong: (done everyday), basic stances.
Basic fitness: (see fitness requirements).

Iron Mantis Martial Arts
White to Blue Belt Curriculum
3rd Chamber, 3 months of training

Bow: attention, set and salute.
Ebay (means begin). Sow (means end).
Horse stance (strikes).

Basic strikes: (fight stance), 1-2-R knee-L knee, 1-2-R low
roundhouse-L middle roundhouse, 1-2-R knee-L high
roundhouse. Shadowbox, heavy bag, mitts, fit-sparring.

Footwork: step forward and back, lunge, stance change.
(mirror drill w/ partner).

Basic stretch: (see stretch requirements).
Basic kicks: cross and propping (fight stance or forward stance).

Mantis boxing: parry drill (stationary and moving),
3-pattern block close-range.
Trapping hands: check and wipe (standing and moving).

Grapple (Jiu-Jitsu): Muay Thai clinch and escape, side-control
escapes.
Solo drills: sprawl, backdrop, technical get-up,
buck and bridge, shrimp, hip heist, rolls.

Gong: (done everyday), walk, jog, or run 1 mile.
Basic fitness: (see fitness requirements).

Iron Mantis Martial Arts
White to Blue Belt Curriculum
4th Chamber, 3 months of training

Bow: attention, set and salute.
Horse stance (kicks)
Ebay (means begin). Sow (means end).

Basic strikes: (Fight stance), 1-2-L front kick-R roundhouse-L
side kick, 1-2-3-L side hammer. Shadowbox, heavy bag, mitts,
fit-sparring

Footwork: stamp step, shuffle back to inside and outside.
Basic stretch: (see stretch requirements)
Basic kicks: groin, side (fight stance or forward stance)

Basic Jim Lim Sau: (Chi Sau / No-Mind).
Stick, follow, yield, adhere, and connect.
(standing horse, chair, bolster, walking horse).

Trapping hands: continuous back fist (standing and moving).

Grapple (Jiu-Jitsu): guillotine (standing/ground)
and defense, guard escapes
Solo drills: sprawl, backdrop, technical get-up,
buck and bridge, shrimp, hip heist, rolls.

Gong: (done everyday), shadowbox 5 minutes.
Basic fitness: (see fitness requirements).

Iron Mantis Martial Arts
Blue to Green belt curriculum
5th Chamber, 3 months of training

Basic strikes: jab-L uppercut-L hook-R cross,
Glover sprawl: backdrop-technical get up-4 P&S.
Controlled sparring.

Footwork: 3-part step, enter angle step, step back at an angle.
(mirror drill).

Standard stretch: (see stretch requirements)
Kicks: close the door, roundhouse, push.

Fundamental form: 8 stance method.

Trapping hands: triple pick-circle punch-crushing.
Playing hands.

Mantis boxing: random 3-way blocking, 3 and 5.
Controlled boxing (1, 2, 4, 6 mats/mat size).

Grapple (Jiu- Jitsu): sprawl (3 levels), scissor sweep, Kimura
sweep. Gi and no-gi rolling.

Gong: 8 Stance Method x 3.

Basic fitness / tools / migong: (see requirements).

Iron Mantis Martial Arts
Blue to Green belt curriculum
6th Chamber, 3 months of training

Basic strikes:
1-2-sprawl, 1-2-liver kick-R knee-R downward hammer.
Controlled sparring.
Footwork: switch stance (3 directions).
Form: 12-punch method.

Elbow set: inside, outside, upward, downward, angles, 3 behind,
rolling, folding, thrusting and throwing.

Standard stretch: (see stretch requirements).
Kicks: back kick, leg sprouting.

Jim Lim Sau: diu jun, got sau.
Trapping hands: reverse-drilling-crushing.
Playing hands.

Mantis boxing: invisible line, fakes and feints.
Controlled boxing (1, 2, 4, 6 mats/mat size).

Grapple (Jiu-Jitsu): Muay Thai clinch over the knee throw,
Americana from mount and side, triangle from guard,
(defenses). Gi and no-gi rolling.

Gong: footwork 5 minutes.
Basic fitness / tools / migong: (see requirements)

Iron Mantis Martial Arts
Blue to Green belt curriculum
7th Chamber, 3 months of training

Basic strikes: 1-2-L front kick-R roundhouse-spinning back kick, 1-2-3-spinning back fist.
Controlled sparring.

Blocks: slant.
Knee set: stationary, stamp, skip, step, switch, flying, side.
.

Standard stretch: (see stretch requirements).

Kicks: hook, inside leg sweep.

Form: 8 Hard Method.

Jim lim Sau: double got sau (stationary and moving).
Playing hands.

Mantis boxing: simultaneous blocks and strikes.
Controlled boxing (1, 2, 4, 6 mats/mat size).

Grapple (Jiu-Jitsu): whizzer, armbar from the guard and side, Kimura from the guard and side, (defenses).
Gi and no-gi rolling.

Gong: feet up 5 minutes.
Basic fitness / tools / migong: (see requirements below).

Iron Mantis Martial Arts
Blue to Green belt curriculum
8th Chamber, 3 months of training

Basic strikes: L hook-R uppercut-L hook-short R cross, body jab-overhand R-L hook, L front kick-cross-L hook-R roundhouse.
Controlled sparring.

Blocks: dragging arm.

Standard stretch: (see stretch requirements).

Form: 12 Keyword Method.

Trapping hands: Eagle Claw drill.
Playing hands.

Mantis boxing: bob, weave, yield and slip.
Controlled boxing (1, 2, 4, 6 mats/mat size).

Grapple (Jiu-Jitsu): body lock double-unders takedowns, body lock escapes, rear-naked choke and defense, scarf hold (2) and escapes (leg hook, spoon and roll).
Gi and no-gi rolling.

Gong: level 2 stretch routine.

Basic fitness / tools / migong: (see requirements).

Iron Mantis Martial Arts
Green to Red belt curriculum
9th Chamber, 3 months of training

Fundamental strikes: double jab-R roundhouse-L hook,
1-2-L roundhouse kick-R spinning hook kick, ice-blitz.

Controlled kickboxing.

Fundamental footwork set: stamp step, shuffle back inside,
shuffle back outside, three part step, step back at an angle, enter
angle step, retreating step and turning step.

Standard stretch: forward stance stretch (3).

Form: 脱战拳 Tue Jein Kuen / exit the battle fist. One of five
battle fist forms of the Ching Woo, a shaolin short fist form.

Jim Lim Sau: Mantis hops - no touch, touch and grab.
Playing hands.

Grapple (Jiu-Jitsu): single-leg takedown, double-leg takedown,
cross chokes, bat choke, arm triangle.
Gi and no-gi, Ground Controlling and Ditang.

Gong: 12 basic stances, 8 stance method, 12 punch method,
8 hard method, 12 keyword method.

Fundamental fitness / tools / migong: (see fitness requirements).

Iron Mantis Martial Arts
Green to Red belt curriculum
10th Chamber, 3 months of training

Fundamental strikes: jab-L hook-R hook-liver punch-L hook, 1-2-switch stance-L roundhouse, 1-2-switch stance-right cross.

Controlled kickboxing.

Advanced footwork: (without bridging).
1. 閃步Sím Bouh Evading Step (any stance or step used to evade an attack). #1 Tiger riding stance change facing forward, #2 Tiger Riding stance change w/ heel kick at a 45 degree angle, #3 Threading the Needle (stepping forward and back), #4 stepping forward and back stance change at a 90 degree angle, #5 stepping forward and back stance change at a 180 degree angle.
2. 走步Jáu Bouh Stalking Step (walking the circle, fist in front).

Standard stretch: toe to sky.
Walking Kicks: (see fundamental kicks and sweeps).
Form: Shaolin Kicking Set.
Grapple (Jiu-Jitsu): Muay Thai clinch knees and elbows, plier choke, ankle lock (standing and ground), kneebar.
Gi and no-gi, Ground Controlling and Ditang.

Gong: Iron shin 5 minutes.
Fundamental fitness / tools / migong: (see fitness requirements).

Iron Mantis Martial Arts
Green to Red belt curriculum
11th Chamber, 3 months of training

Fundamental strikes:
Triple hook-R elbow-push-spinning back kick,
1-2-liver kick-1-2-3-Thai clinch knees, blitz-jumping knee.

Controlled sanda.

Standard stretch: forward fold.

Standing kick set: 6", cross, leg sprouting, propping, groin,
snap, roundhouse, side, outside crescent,
jumping inside crescent, back, push.

Trapping hands: triple pick-crushing-circle-cast and reel.
Playing hands.

Grapple (Jiu-Jitsu): arm drags (standing and ground), Umaplata.

Gi and no-gi, Ground Controlling and Ditang.

Gong: Sitting qigong (18 to 36 double breaths)

Fundamental fitness / tools / migong: (see fitness requirements)

Iron Mantis Martial Arts
Green to Red belt curriculum
12th Chamber, 3 months of training

Fundamental strikes: 1-2-3-weave-L hook-R elbow-takedown, L arm leg catch-cross-L hook, 1-2-fake low R roundhouse-superman.

Controlled MMA.

16 Attacking Points: (*8 attacking / 8 non-attacking*).
Eyes, nose, jaw, throat, temples, ears, neck, cervical spine, solar plexus, stomach, ribs, liver, groin, knee, shin, kidneys.

Standard stretch: butterfly stretch.

Form: 12 Linking Palms.

Trapping hands: (single arm) diu jun bung da.
Playing hands.

Grapple (Jiu-Jitsu): standing key-lock, triple triangle.
Gi and no-gi, Ground Controlling and Ditang.

Gong: 12 Standing kicks x 3.

Fundamental fitness / tools / migong: (see fitness requirements).

鐵 螂 Fundamental Kicks & Sweeps

(walking forward & stepping back)

Leg sprouting
6 inch
Shin (cross and propping)
Groin
Close door
Push kick
Heart piercing
Throat piercing
Front rising (3 ways)
Snap
Crescent (inside and outside)
Whip kick
Double slap kick
Single slap kick (walking and jump kick)
Lotus
Roundhouse
Side
Hook
Tornado
Whirlwind
Butterfly
Sweeps (forward, back and combinations)
Ditang (hand strikes, kicks and sweeps)

Iron Mantis Martial Arts
Red to Brown belt curriculum
13th Chamber, 3 months of training

Fundamental strikes: jab-jab-feint-cross-L hook-R leg kick-L hook, Jab-fake cross-2 o'clock with cross-L hook-takedown.

MMA sparring.

Standard stretch: splits (3).

Ditang fundamentals: 1-12 (see ditang).

Form: 12 Mantis Method.

Mantis boxing: offense without bridging (see Mantis Boxing / MB theories).

MB sparring.

Grapple (Jiu-Jitsu): leg catch takedowns and escapes, paper-cutter.

Gi and no-gi, Ground Controlling and Ditang.

Gong: all fundamental forms.

Fitness / tools / migong: (see fitness requirements).

Iron Mantis Martial Arts
Red to Brown belt curriculum
14th Chamber, 3 months of training

Strikes: jab-slip-L backfist-Muay Thai clinch-knees-elbows, Wide L hook-R Whip kick-R side kick.

MMA sparring.

Standard stretch: butterfly stance.

Fundamental block set: *(solo and with partner)*
hook in/out, Mantis Claw in/out, Eagle Claw in/out, slant block, dragging arm.

Mantis boxing: counter theory 1-8 (see Mantis Boxing / MB theories).

MB sparring.

Grapple (Jiu-Jitsu): Ezekiel choke (standing and ground).

Gi and no-gi, Ground Controlling and Ditang.

Gong: Iron body 5 minutes.

Fitness / tools / migong: (see fitness requirements)

Iron Mantis Martial Arts
Red to Brown belt curriculum
15th Chamber, 3 months of training

Fundamental punches: 1-2-3-4-shovel-circle-backfist-hammerfist. (Fundamental punch set).

MMA sparring.

Trapping hands: Mantis Plucks Pearls.

Playing hands.

Standard stretch: elbow to toe.

Fundamental Sanda drills: 1-15 (see sanda).

Form: Shaolin Qigong Breath Set.

Mantis boxing: bridging theory 1-6 (see Mantis Boxing / MB theories).

MB sparring.

Gong: footwork 5 minutes.

Fitness / tools / migong: (see fitness requirements).

Iron Mantis Martial Arts
Red to Brown belt curriculum
16th Chamber, 3 months of training

Advanced strike set: eye plunder, thrusting palm, tile palm, falling palm, back hand, ear claw, wrist thrust, wrist swing.

Playing hands.

Standard stretch: Iron Bridge. Rolls, dive rolls & break falls.

Fundamental Jim Lim Sau drills:
Empty strikes, empty blocks, circle out of grabs.
(shown and explained in solo drills and in the trapping hand drills).

Mantis boxing: kicking theory 1-8
(see Mantis Boxing / MB theories).

Mantis Boxing sparring.

Gong: 10 Fundamental Forms:
(12 Basic Stances, 8 Stance Method, 12 Punch Method, 8 Hard Method, 12 Keyword Method (12 Keys), Evading Attack, Shaolin Kicking Set, 12 Linking Palms, 12 Mantis Method, Shaolin Qigong Breath Set).

Fitness / tools / migong: (see fitness requirements).

As a Brown Belt you are in between the Four Levels and the Ten Degrees; believe it or not, many get lost in this area. I refer to this area as *The Void*. This is a time of reviewing, this time should not be longer than 12 months but it can be shorter. A time of training, assisting if possible, and further understanding of the curriculum. In the martial arts world, Brown Belts are notoriously the most rowdy, aggressive and hungry students in the school, trying to prove they deserve the Black Belt. It's the goal of the student and the teacher to achieve the black belt 5 years from start date. Write the dates down for both teacher and student. Set those goals!

As a Brown Belt you've learned Levels 1 & 2, aka the Iron Mantis basics, and Levels 3 & 4, aka the Iron Mantis fundamentals. Together, the basics and the fundamentals form the Iron Mantis Foundation. Now is the time to work towards a better understanding of everything you have learned. If possible, teach a friend or family member for free or assist classes under an Iron Mantis Coach or Sifu. This will help you in more ways than you realize, and this is where you will better understand the concept of *service.*

Do your *Gong* everyday to earn each stripe to Black Belt, this practice is golden and essential. Once you've earned 4 stripes on your Brown Belt you are eligible to test for your Black Belt and a date should be set by your teacher / Sifu. Black Belt tests must have an Iron Mantis Sifu in attendance and may include special guests. Review all levels of the curriculum, take notes, and ask questions. Study recommended reading daily.

Brown to Black Belt
Review, study and train.

The Doctrine of the Voidness:
The things that are seen are temporal; the things that are unseen are eternal.

Gong:
An exercise or list of exercises to be completed daily preferably at the same each day. This daily discipline is done until the student receives the next belt stripe or the next belt rank. Traditionally a Gong is 100 days of practice. This discipline leads to one's Kundalini Yoga Sadhana.

Brown Belt 1 stripe: full Migong practice
(arms, palms, elbows, knees, shins, calves, head and body)

Brown Belt 2 stripes: Get caught up on all the recommended reading and meditate at least 20 minutes a day.

Brown Belt 3 stripes: sitting Qigong (opening the four gates - breath, vision, hearing, and emptiness)

Brown Belt 4 stripes: All the Fundamental Forms 3 times each back to back.

Iron Mantis
Ditang fundamentals / ground fighting

Break falls (with get-up).
Rolls with break falls & get-up.
Add kicks with get-up.
Rotating on the ground & on back.
Ground kicks on shields & pads.
Ground takedowns with feet & sweeps.
Feet on knees and hook knees (rotating).
Feet on knee and hip takedown.
Fast hip drills. Grappling one up one down.
Controlled sparring one up one down w/ shin pads.
Sparring with shin pads & gloves, start one up one down.
Freestyle sparring focusing on Ditang.

Iron Mantis
Sanda / Kickboxing drills

Warm-up: Shadow boxing.
jab, cross, head hook, body hook, uppercut, head shield with body strikes, body conditioning, push kicks, back roundhouse (shield & check), front roundhouse (shield & check), side kick, cross kick, propping.

1. one technique drilling
2. build-ups drilling
3. spar w/ build-ups
4. freestyle sparring with takedowns (sanda)

Fundamentals of Iron Mantis Boxing
Mantis Boxing Theories

Offense without bridging
1. Effective combinations
2. Using angles for attack
3. Moving to position of advantage
4. Range manipulation
5. Destroy the limb
6. Exploit a door to open a door
7. Vary the attack
8. Fake/faint

Counter Theory
1. Simultaneous block and counter
2. Counter with opposite
3. Set a trap with false opening
4. Step off line and counter
5. Change to nullify
6. Cover and wait for an opening
7. Trading theory
8. Destroying the limb

Bridging Theory
1. Fake/faint
2. Distraction
3. Broken rhythm
4. Timing
5. Angle change for advantage

Kicking Theory
1. Kicking with no movement
2. Kicking followed by hands
3. Rear leg kick to advance
4. Kick low to open high
5. Fake hand, use leg
6. Double kick to confuse
7. Kick when enemy advances
8. Kick when the hands are engaged

Basic, Fundamental and Advanced Strikes

Effective combinations
(fight stance), jab, cross, jab-cross, L hook,
1-2-3-weave L & R.
4 punches and sprawl,
L hook-cross, 1-2-R front kick.
1-2-R knee-L knee, 1-2-R low roundhouse-L middle
roundhouse, 1-2-R knee-L high roundhouse.
1-2-L front kick-R roundhouse-L side kick, 1-2-3-L side
hammer. Jab-L uppercut-L hook-R cross,
Glover sprawl: backdrop-technical get up-4 P&S.
1-2-sprawl, 1-2-liver kick-R knee-R downward hammer.
1-2-L front kick-R roundhouse-spinning back kick,
1-2-3-spinning back fist.
L hook-R uppercut-L hook-short R cross, body jab-overhand
R-L hook, L front kick-cross-L hook-R roundhouse.
double jab-R roundhouse-L hook,
1-2-L roundhouse kick-R spinning hook kick, ice-blitz.
 jab-L hook-R hook-liver punch-L hook,
1-2-switch stance-L roundhouse,
1-2-switch stance-right cross.
triple hook-R elbow-push-spinning back kick,
1-2-liver kick-1-2-3-Thai clinch knees, blitz-jumping knee.
1-2-3-weave-L hook-R. elbow-takedown,
L arm leg catch-cross-L hook,
1-2-fake low R roundhouse-superman.
jab-jab-feint-cross-L hook-R leg kick-L hook,
Jab-fake cross-2 o'clock with cross-L hook-takedown.
jab-slip L back fist-Thai clinch-knees-elbows, Wide L hook-R
whip kick-R side kick.

Basic Mantis Boxing drills
1. 3 pattern block
2. Mirror drill
3. Focus theory
4. Random 3 way blocking
5. 3 and 5
6. Invisible line
7. Fakes and feints
8. Bob & weave, slip and fade

鐵 螂 Work Sets

Basic footwork set
shuffle forward, back, inside, outside, step forward and back, lunge, stance change. Circle walking.

Fundamental footwork set
stamp step, shuffle back inside, shuffle back outside, three part step, step back at an angle, enter angle step, retreating step and turning step. switch stance (3 directions).

Advanced footwork set
(offense without bridging)
1. 閃步Sím Bouh Evading Step (any stance or step used to evade an attack)
2. 走步Jáu Bouh Stalking Step

Basic blocking set
3-pattern block (long, mid and close range)

Fundamental blocking set
hook in/out, Mantis Claw in/out, Eagle Claw in/out, slant block, dragging arm.

Fundamental striking set
jab-cross-hook-uppercut-shovel-circle-backfist-hammerfist.

Advanced striking set
eye plunder, thrusting palm, tile palm, falling palm, back hand, ear claw, wrist thrust, wrist swing.

8 Elbows set
inside, outside, upward, downward, angles, 3 behind, rolling, folding, thrusting and throwing.

8 Knees set
stationary, stamp, skip, step, switch, flying, side.

12 Standing kicks set
6 inch, cross, leg sprouting, propping, groin, snap, roundhouse, side, outside crescent, jumping inside crescent, back, push.

16 Attacking points

(Shaolin 8 attacking & 8 non-attacking points)

eyes, nose, jaw, throat, temples, ears, neck, cervical spine, solar plexus, stomach, ribs, liver, groin, knee, shin, kidneys.

鐵 螂 Ditang Jiu Jitsu /Grappling Fundamentals

Wrestling and ground controlling

Headlock defense, swim drill, over the knee takedown, mount escapes, attacks from the top and bottom, Muay Thai clinch and escape, side-control escapes, guillotine (standing/ground) and defense, guard escapes, sprawl (3 levels), scissor sweep, Kimura sweep, Muay Thai clinch over the knee throw, Americana from mount and side, triangle from guard, (defenses), whizzer, armbar from the guard and side, Kimura from the guard and side, (defenses), body lock double-unders takedowns, body lock escapes, rear-naked choke and defense, scarf hold (2) and escapes (leg hook, spoon and roll), single-leg takedown, double-leg takedown, cross chokes, bat choke, arm triangle,

Muay Thai clinch knees and elbows, plier choke,
ankle lock (standing and ground), kneebar, arm drags (standing
and ground), Umaplata, standing key-lock, triple triangle, leg
catch takedowns and escapes, paper-cutter, Ezekiel choke.
Solo drills: sprawl, backdrop, technical get-up,
buck and bridge, shrimp, (also done with a partner).

Trapping hands *(mindfulness)*

Check and wipe (standing and moving),
continuous back fist (standing and moving),
triple pick-circle punch-crushing,
reverse-drilling-crushing,
triple pick-crushing-circle-cast and reel,
diu jun bung da (single arm),
Mantis plucks pearls.

Chi Sau *(no-mind drills & flow)*

Sticking, following, yielding, adhering, connecting.

Jim Lim Sau *(Mantis Sticky Hands)*

Diu jun, got sau.

Double got sau (stationary and moving).

Mantis hops – no touch, touch and grab.

Empty strikes, empty blocks, circle out of grabs.

Fundamental Fighting Theories

The fundamental theories are general truths about fighting that serve a defensive or offensive purpose. By following and understanding these theories you will understand the fundamental objective of fighting. To hit and not be hit.

1. *Root Theory* – The root theory is the ability to ground yourself and have a solid foundation. This is important in preventing the enemy from knocking you to the ground, and in generating power in strikes, knocking the enemy to the ground. In rooting, stance, body position, weight distribution and proper movement are key.

2. *Power Theory* – This is a method of generating power through the use of body mechanics. It enables you to generate more power than an isolated strike, like just punching using the muscular strength of the arm. This becomes critical when getting older or when someone does not have much physical strength.

3. *Six Harmonies* – Keep the shoulders over the hips, elbows over the knees, and hands with the feet. Don't lean forward or to the sides. Elbows and knees work together in close quarters combat. Hands and feet move together.

4. *One in / One out Theory* – This theory is aimed at keeping a guard at all times. When you extend to block, the non-blocking hand is still in a guard position; when you punch, the non-punching hand is still in the guard position. After punching, the hand returns to the guard position. This way you will not open yourself to a counter-attack. Where you punch will determine the position of the guard hand. This has also been called the "guard hand theory."

5. *Rule of Three* – The rule of three is a principal based on the fact that the enemy has two arms as do you. In principle, you could throw two strikes and the enemy would be able to perform two improper blocks and would be okay because he also has two arms. The mistake, or improper blocks, would not matter until a third attack is thrown and the error in blocking would show itself in the enemy's inability to block the third attack. The rule of three means that more than two errors in blocking will be revealed by throwing combinations, a more effective attack.

6. *Focus Theory* – This is the tactic of using peripheral vision when fighting to detect movement from the opponent. Peripheral vision is much more effective because it is connected to the subconscious mind. Your acute vision is connected to your conscious mind and is slower. The main

challenge is to learn to trigger peripheral vision and to stay in that mode. This is achieved by focusing on a spot that does not physically exist, such as a spot in front of the enemy's chest.

7. *Invisible Line* – The focus theory is so effective that it will cause you to see all movement. In effect, it may cause you to react when there is not an attack or a false attack, an example being when someone uses the tactic of fakes and faints. To prevent this from happening you set an invisible line in your mind. This imaginary line or wall is in front of your forward hand; you train yourself to not respond to any attacks that do not cross this line. By practicing this you will train your mind not to react to false attacks.

8. *Door Theory* – This theory involves dividing the body with imaginary lines vertically and horizontally. This creates a series of zones also referred to as doors, or "men" in Chinese. The general objective is to attack or open to attack the enemy's doors and to keep your doors closed to attack. Keeping your doors closed involves the theories already discussed as well as others. Opening doors will be covered in later levels.

9. *Zone Theory* – The zone theory is designed to minimize exposure to attacks and maximize efficiency in blocking. The zone theory teaches us how to maintain a strong defense when blocking. Zone defense aims to keep the blocking arm in a zone as much as possible. By moving as little as possible it will prevent you from creating openings. A good rule is to not move a defensive action more than one "door" over from its position. Anything more would make it difficult to return to a strong guard position.

10. *Centerline Theory* – The centerline is an imaginary vertical line running down the center of the enemies' body. By "capturing" or controlling the center you are able to control the opponent's body because it is the pivot point. The centerline is also important because of all its targets, like the groin, stomach, solar plexus, throat, and head.

11. *Range Theory* – Range is a critical factor in fighting, it affects a number of things, including tactics and techniques. Controlling the range often determines success and failure. In close-range fighting, the arms must be held closer to the body and the angles of strikes become more important. Learn all ranges, and learn to maintain the proper range for you.

12. *Effective Strike Theory* – This is the theory of striking the body's vulnerable targets to maximize effectiveness. The traditional targets were called the eight attacking points and the eight non-attacking points. Sifu Tony Puyot did years of research with both Western and Eastern doctors and countless high-level martial artists. He was unable to get any understanding, logic, or validity for the traditional targets listed. He reformatted this area of training into the eight head targets and the eight body targets. These are naturally vulnerable targets of the human body. There are other effective targets that we attack, however these are the primary ones used.

Sticky Hands / Trapping Hands / Playing Hands

The art of chi sau, or "no-mind/sticky hands," is a term widely used in the Wing Chun circles and tui shou, "push hands" of Tai Chi Chuan; Eagle Claw Kung Fu also has similar training. The no-mind/sticky hands aspect or training is a part of Iron Mantis Martial Arts. In Iron Mantis, jim lim sau is known as "trapping hands," and is very similar, but with its own guiding techniques and principles. Jim lim sau allows a practitioner to elevate his or her techniques through the skill of touch. This skill can allow one to "measure" and "listen" to his/her partner or adversary's intentions. Our way of "playing hands" is very similar to that of Yin Baugua Zhang.

In the beginning of acquainting yourself with jim lim sau, one must understand chi sau and learn to follow the other's movement without leading. This is done with great patience and complete trust in the sifu's guidance. Much time has to be taken to slow one's movements, calm the spirit and fully "hear" one's opponent. This "no-mind" calmness combined with jim lim sau can eventually be carried into full-speed, full-power combat. Jim lim sau is a piece of the Iron Mantis puzzle. Like strength and flexibility, this skill is an attribute for the Iron Mantis practitioner. Other important essentials to remember in jim lim sau include staying relaxed yet "full" and constantly moving with no wasted movements. This skill of trapping hands is also used in Folk Wrestling, referred to as "hand fighting," and in Judo and Brazilian Jiu Jitsu referred to as "grip fighting" and is a highly effective skill which determines the outcome of success and failure.

Playing hands combines these pieces in a smooth controlled manner of practice. Other styles like Karate and Muay Thai have their own version of this practice which we refer to as playing hands. Our focus is first to move slowly, focusing on our breath, then slowly speed up and slowly back down when needed. There's a time for power speed and explosive movements and a time to break things down to better understand them - all things tested. Playing hands is a methodical way of sparring designed to increase skills without damaging one another, similar to rolling in Jiu Jitsu. When we are stressed we cannot problem solve so we keep it playful and in time we carry this mindset into more stressful situations. It's a process, one that takes time to achieve. There are no shortcuts, many times shortcuts end up being the long way; time is precious and should not be wasted. The goal is to get a student to a high level of skill as quickly as possible without getting in a hurry.

In our Ditang Jiu Jitsu practice we have "smooth jazz" drills to help develop this soft touch while practicing ground fighting.

The focus becomes the flow and going with the opponent, very much like a dance. This dance is a harmony of movement, a type of controlled chaos, with behavior so unpredictable as to appear random, owing to great sensitivity to small changes. These esoteric practices have been handed down for centuries and are honored to this day. We are upholding tradition for modern times.

For students, only by placing much emphasis on the training of the system's techniques and drills, understanding concepts and theories, and working long hours on internal training and fitness, effective combinations, and ground fighting will the practitioner ascend to the highest level. For teachers, only by placing much emphasis on forms and how to apply them correctly can one hope to accomplish the highest level of proficiency in the art of Iron Mantis Martial Arts. Jim lim sau enables a practitioner to actually use the techniques from the forms and apply them successfully. The forms hold the keys to the knowledge handed down from masters to students in our lineage of 400 years. Remember the rules governing wushu: when you get hurt, don't let your opponent know; use deception, and don't use the same technique all the time. In combat pay attention to controlling the opponent's elbow, also known as "the body handle." When grabbed, yield and twist, and use circular motions in the direction of the force; follow then attack. Collapsing techniques are used offensively and defensively.

Jim lim sau heightens the martial artist's sense of awareness and increases contact reflexes. One purpose is to sense for centerline mistakes. Repetition, time and hard work on mantis boxing, trapping hands, takedowns and takedown defense, ditang jiu jitsu and knowing the forms builds a strong foundation. Our forms include yoga, qigong, tanglangquan and taijiquan.

88 Chambers of Iron Mantis

Each Chamber to Black Belt is 3 months of training
Basic Training (2 years) - 8 chambers
Fundamental Training (2 years) - 8 chambers
The Void (1 year of reviewing and preparing for BB test)
Black Belt (total 16 chambers / 5 years)

Each Chamber beyond BB is an area of focus

Black Belt Coach:
1st degree (3 years) - 8 chambers
2nd degree (3 years) - 8 chambers
3rd degree (3 years) - 8 chambers

Black Belt Sifu:
4th degree (5 years) - 8 chambers
5th degree (5 years) - 8 chambers
6th degree (5 years) - 8 chambers

Black Belt Master:
7th degree (10 years) - 8 chambers
8th degree (10 years) - 8 chambers
9th degree (10 years) - 8 chambers

10th degree Grandmaster - 88 chambers

Iron Mantis Fitness
An outline for IM Strength & Conditioning

Mind - Body - Spirit

Iron Mantis Fitness
Basic requirements – Level 1
White to Blue Belt

White belt 1 stripe: 800 meter row in ≤ 5 minutes, 10 push-ups in ≤ 1 minute, 10 squats in ≤ 1 minute, 10 sit-ups in ≤ 1 minute, ½ Black Jack in ≤ 10 minutes, horse stance for 1 minute

White belt 2 stripes: 800 meter row in ≤ 4 minutes 30 seconds, 15 push-ups in ≤ 1 minute, 15 squats in ≤ 1 minute, 15 sit-ups in ≤ 1 minute, Black Jack in ≤ 20 minutes, horse stance for 1.5 minutes

White belt 3 stripes: 800 meter row in ≤ 4 minutes, 20 push-ups in ≤ 1 minute, 20 squats in ≤ 1 minute, 20 sit-ups in ≤ 1 minute, Black Jack in ≤ 18 minutes, horse stance for 2 minutes

White belt 4 stripes: SPT warm-ups, 20 box jumps in ≤ 1 minute, 5 pull-ups in ≤ 1 minute, 6 bag slams in ≤ 1 minute, 12 burpees in ≤ 1 minute, Black Jack in ≤ 15 minutes, horse stance for 2.5 minute

Black Jack: 20-1… 1-20, push-ups and squats

Iron Mantis Fitness
Basic requirements – Level 2
Blue to Green Belt

Blue *belt 1 stripe*: 22 box jumps in ≤ 1 minute,
7 pull-ups in ≤ 1 minute, 7 bag slams in ≤ 1 minute,
14 burpees in ≤ 1 minute, Black Jack in ≤ 12 minute,
horse stance for 3 minutes

Blue belt 2 stripes: 24 box jumps in ≤ 1 minute,
8 pull-ups in ≤ 1 minute, 8 bag slams in ≤ 1 minute,
16 burpees in ≤ 1 minute, Black Jack in ≤ 10 minute,
horse stance for 3.5 minutes

Blue belt 3 stripes: 26 box jumps in ≤ 1 minute,
10 pull-ups in ≤ 1 minute, 250 meter row in ≤ 1 minute,
18 burpees in ≤ 1 minute, horse stance for 4 minutes

Blue belt 4 stripes: 15 Ernies in ≤ 1 minute, 250 meter row
in ≤ 55 seconds, 50 doubles in ≤ 2 minute or 50 burpees
≤ 3 minute (*if you can't do doubles*), horse stance for 4.5
minutes

Ernies: Burpee box jumps

Iron Mantis Fitness
Basic tools, strength training and migong / body conditioning

1. Iron arm on sandbag.
2. Iron palm (1-2-3 / overwhelming palm).
3. Sand jars / shot-puts (Tiger Claw).
4. Forearm / ankle weights (forms).
5. Iron shin (kicking heavy bag with full-force).
6. Sand bags (elbows / knees).
7. Push-ups (knuckles x10, 5 palms x 5, tiger tail x 10, finger & thumb x 3).
8. Six inch raises (up / down, open / close, flutter kick, scissor kicks, bicycle, belly strikes with fist, back hypers x 10).

Iron Mantis Fitness
Basic goals

Squats - 50
Push-ups - 10
Static hang - 30
Kettlebell or dumbbell swings - 25 (25#)
400 meter run - 2:04 or less
Deadlift - 3/4 bodyweight
Standing press - 1/4 bodyweight
Plank hold - 30 seconds
Wall ball - 25 (15# / 20#)

800 meter run - 4:20 or less
500 meter row - women 2:20, men 1:55
Dips - 3
Pull-ups - 3
L-sit - 10 seconds
2000 meter row - women 9:50, men 8:10
Christine - 15 minutes or less (3 rounds for time: 500 meter row, 12 deadlifts, 21 box jumps)
One mile run - 9 minutes or less

Iron Mantis Fitness
Fundamental requirements - Level 3
Green to Red Belt

Green belt 1 stripe: 800 meter run in ≤ 4 minutes, 100 wall balls in ≤ 6 minutes, 400 meter / 21 elephants / pull-ups 12 reps × 3 sets ≤ 17 minutes, horse stance for 5 minutes,
1 pull-up and add a pull-up each minute –
minimum of 8 pull-ups in the eighth minute

Green belt 2 stripes: 800 meter run in ≤ 3 minutes 50 seconds, 30 box jumps ≤ 1 minute, thrusters & pull-ups 21-15-9 ≤ 17 minutes, horse stance for 5.5 minutes, 5 minutes of man-makers, Pedestal x 10

Green belt 3 stripes: 800 meter run in ≤ 3 minutes 45 seconds, 45 burpees in ≤ 3 minutes, 100 sit-ups in ≤ 3 minutes,
10 calorie row in ≤ 30 seconds, 400 meter / 21 elephants / pull-ups 12 reps × 3 sets ≤ 16 minutes, Card Game in ≤ 12

minutes, horse stance for 6 minutes,   Pedestal x 15

Green belt 4 stripes: 100 push-ups in ≤ 3 minutes, 1600 meter row in ≤ 7 minutes, 20 pull-ups / 30 push-ups / 40 sit-ups / 50 squats - five rounds - each for time - average ≤ 6 minutes per round, horse stance for 7 minutes, Pedestal x 20

Iron Mantis Fitness
Fundamental tools & migong

1. Iron shin (rolling).
2. Iron body basics (head, torso, calves, thighs).
3. Iron pole set (wrist and forearm strength).
4. Cement pads (Eagle Claw grip).
5. Sticks taped together (Iron body tapping).
6. 3 poles to twist (Eagle Claw grip).
7. Double Steel Whips and Double Hammers (heavy weapons drills).
8. Pistols / single leg squats (100 each side).

Iron Mantis Fitness
Fundamental requirements – Level 4
Red to Brown Belt

Red belt 1 stripe: 800 meter row in ≤ 3 minutes, 22 head kicks in ≤ 1 minute, 12 pull-ups ≤ 1 minute, Jackie in ≤ 18 minutes – (1000 meter row – 50 thrusters of 45#, 30 pull-ups), horse stance for 8 minutes

Red belt 2 stripes: 800 meter row in ≤ 2 minutes 50 seconds, 15 Ernies in ≤ 1 minute, Halcyon in ≤ 15 minutes – (800 meter row, 800 meter run, 100 push-ups, 100 sit-ups), PT for Convicts, horse stance for 9 minutes

Red belt 3 stripes: 30 clean & jerks in ≤ 5 minutes, 13 pull-ups in ≤ 1 minute, 1 mile run in ≤ 8 minute, 20 burpees in ≤ 1 minute, horse stance for 10 minutes

Red *belt 4 stripes:* Strength & Conditioning fundamentals: Warm-ups, static stretch, dynamic warmups, dynamic stretches, general strength with medicine ball, pedestal x20.

Iron Mantis Fitness
Brown to Black Belts

Brown Belt 1 stripe: Jumping rope 3 times a week, lifting three days a week, BT WOD in between lifting days, three days a week spar, roll and play hands. Tackle the Fitness Goals.

Brown Belt 2 stripes: Sprints 3 times a week, lifting three days a week, BT WOD in between lifting days, three days a week spar, roll and play hands. Tackle the Fitness Goals.

Brown Belt 3 stripes: Rowing 3 times a week, lifting three days a week, BT WOD in between lifting days, three days a week spar, roll and play hands. Tackle the Fitness Goals.

Brown Belt 4 stripes: Stationary bike 3 times a week, lifting three days a week, BT WOD in between lifting days, three days a week spar, roll and play hands. Tackle the Fitness Goals.

An 8-count push-up is a squat thrust with 2 push-ups

Brown belts are expected to teach martial arts and fitness classes and assist in special events while preparing for their Black belt exam.

螳 螂 Fundamental tools & migong

1. Iron arms / shins (hanging sandbag)
2. Iron arm two person drills
3. Iron palm, fist, ridge hand
4. Barbell (rolling arms & walking the horse)
5. Wooden dummy 3-star Iron Arm
6. Bricks and plum flower poles for stances
8. Metal staff and Horse Chopper (drills)

鐵 螂 Fundamental fitness goals

Squats - 100
Squat - 1 rep with body weight
Push-ups - 30
Bench press - 1 rep with body weight
Rope climb - 13 ft rope climb 2 times
V-ups - 30
Dumbbell snatch - 30 each arm, men 50#, women 30#
400 meter run - 1:34 or less
Deadlift - 1 1/2 bodyweight
Standing press - 1/2 body weight

Handstand hold - 1 minute
Power clean - 3/4 bodyweight
Hanging knees to elbow - 15 (no kip)
Thrusters - 45 reps at 1/2 body weight
800 meter row - 3:20 or less
500 meter row - women 2:00 minutes, men 1:45 minutes
Dips - 20
Dip - 1 with 1/3 bodyweight
Pull-ups - 20
Muscle-up - 1
L-sits - 30 seconds
2000 meter row - women 8:50, men 7:30
Power snatch - 1/2 bodyweight
Helen - 11:30 (3 rounds for time - 400 meter run, 21 KB or DB swings, 12 pull-ups)
1 mile run - 7 minutes

Diet and Nutrition for IM athletes

Beginning with breakfast, eat 4-6 small meals throughout the day, every 2.5 - 3.5 hours. Each meal should consist of a lean protein source (20-30 grams), 1-2 veggies sources (5 different colored ones each day), and 1 fruit choice (4-5 different colored ones each day).

Decrease sugar intake and bad fat intake drastically, and increase water intake to 1 gallon per day. This will keep blood sugar levels more stable, lessening surges and drops, and providing a more constant energy level throughout the day. Along with exercise, these steps also help increase lean tissue development, raise testosterone levels, increase HGH levels, and decrease body fat levels. Lastly, add the correct supplements, Chinese and Ayurvedic herbs to your diet, and you'll think you're on rocket fuel.

Iron Mantis stretch routines, forms, qigong, tai chi, yoga and meditation are referred to as our self-therapy practices. On top of these, utilize our network of wellness professionals. These professionals specialize in Acupuncture, Sports Therapy, Chiropractic Therapy, and more. Practice recovery daily, work on diet, nutritional timing, supplements, water intake and adequate rest and sleep. Do cleanses seasonally and when necessary a fast.

Basic Rotational Stretch
Head – circles, up and down, ear to shoulder, looking
Shoulders – arm swing circles, crane's beak
Elbows – circles and tea cups
Arms – straight out - small circles
Wrists – circles, shake
Chest – chain breakers, twist
Waist – reach towards ankles, relax arms to the side and twist, slap kidneys and shoulders, circle hips
Hips – knees up and out
Knees – together and circle both directions with palms lightly touching knees, crane stance knees in a circle / back and front / ankles in a circle
Ankles – palms rise and fall rocking back/forth, ankle twist

Basic Static Stretch

Hanging middle splits – elbows hanging / palms on the ground / elbows on the ground / head to right knee / head to left knee / grab ankles head between, palms down, walk feet in hips side-to-side, walk feet together head down, slowly roll up and arch back. Spider stretch – palms down, elbows down, straighten both legs head to knee, kneeling heel to bottom. Walk out the calves.

Standard *Static Stretch*

Forward – front toe forward and back ball of foot, hands on the waist, back straight and sink waist below knee, head up. Next, slide feet apart.

Snake in the grass – foot flat on the ground with knee over the toe and other leg straight to one side with calf on the ground and toe pointing up. Next, one hand behind the straight leg and 1) head to knee, 2) chin to shin, 3) head to toe.

Side to sides – both feet flat, shift to one side with the other leg straight. 1) palms flat on the ground, 2) grab ankles, and 3) hands on the waist. Next, 1) sword chop, 2) mantis turns.

Middle splits – 1) hands on thighs, 2) palms on the ground, 3) elbows on the ground, 4) chest to ground, 5) sit back and forth. *Side splits* – back knee on the ground, straighten back leg push front foot forward. 1) one hand on each side, back straight, head up, 2) rock from side to side, 3) hands on the thighs, 4) head down in front.

Knees to the side – back flat on the ground, pick up hips and turn on one side. Keep 90 degrees at hips and knees angled, with arms out to each side. Lift ribs and turn until both shoulders and ribs are flat on the ground.

Sitting head to toe – 1) grab feet, 2) head to knees, 3) chest and stomach flat, 4) grab toes, lift heels 5) elbows to shins/floor.

Butterfly – grab ankles, pull in and press down on your thighs with your elbows.

Iron Bridge – walk hands close to feet, straighten arms, rock forward, one leg and arm up at a time.

Knees to chest – lay on your back and hug your knees. Roll back and forth to massage your back. Roll up onto your feet without crossing your legs.

Seven-Star – back knee over toe and front leg straight. 1) grab foot, 2) head to knee, 3) chin to shin, 4) elbow to toe, 5) head to toe, 6) kiss the toe.

鐵 螂 *Strong People are Harder to Kill*

Shorthand Techniques of the Seven Star Mantis

Seven Star Praying Mantis Kung Fu is known for its use of the diu sau (mantis claw) combined with the fast, agile footwork of the monkey. Seven Star Praying Mantis is a complete system which uses hand, arm, and body strikes like tung choi (straight punch), bung choi (crashing down), huen choi (circular strike), pek choi (hammer fist), jeung (palm strikes), elbows, shoulders, hips, and knees. Mantis practitioners use these hand strikes along with many kicks such as chau tui (leg-sprouting with seven star stance), jaat tui (leg bumping with shin kick), bai muh tui (closing door with toe kick), and chyun sam tui (heart piercing with heel kick). The mantis system also emphasizes techniques such as ou lou choi (triple pick), yul jam (waist-chopping), sweeps, rolls, pressure points, chin-na (joint locks), and jim lim sau (sticky hands). The mantis principles guide the execution of all techniques, and though the Mantis System has long, middle, and short range fighting theories, it is known for using shorthand techniques.

The Mantis principles are guiding factors that can help complete a practitioner. The system contains the twelve keyword formula of attack and defense, eight attacking points and eight non-attacking points, seven long and eight short techniques, five external elements and five internal elements, four principles of movement, inner and outer gates, and the eight hard and twelve soft principles. Of the principal categories, the twelve soft are usually the most difficult to master.

If one is learning the kuens (forms) properly, then they are already practicing the foundation of these principles. Many people can understand the eight hard principles, but lack the patience and perseverance to fully comprehend and apply the twelve soft. There are many theories that explain the importance of the soft principles in the martial arts, such as "the soft overcomes the hard," "flow like water" and "iron wrapped in cotton." These sayings carry weight, and have meaning. The yin yang theory further explains the balance between complementary opposites. Ultimately, there is only one way to learn Iron Mantis and that's on the floor with the masters. Whether in a hallway, an empty building, or in a park, it makes no difference. Stepping into the Iron Mantis circle is like no other.

Seven Star Mantis is known as an external system mainly because of the way a practitioner trains in body conditioning such as iron arm, iron palm, and iron body. The way the forms are practiced also shows the external use of energy in the hard, fast, explosive movements. However, Seven Star Mantis is very internal in its usage of breath control, chi sau and fighting techniques. Mantis forms flow by the practitioner relaxing during transitions and linking the techniques with smooth movements. The internal and external are combined with Iron Body Conditioning when practicing the internal sets such as The Eighteen Lo Han Hei Gong. The internal forms build strength and give the martial artist insight of how to develop power in the techniques. Because of the difficulty involved in mastering the soft principles of Mantis, demonstrations of these principles are usually only seen from high-level practitioners behind closed doors. Fortunately, now with the internet, many of us can see these rare demonstrations.

The principles can all be found and explained in techniques. The forms hold the answers and the secrets of Mantis Kung Fu. To unlock the secrets in the forms and have the questions answered, one must practice the forms handed down in one's lineage. Once a Mantis practitioner has understood the basic and intermediate forms and the applications, the Sifu can bring the principles to light. After years of practicing the forms, the student realizes he or she has been teaching his or her body the principles by constant repetition. The proper adherence to the principles while training with one's Kung Fu brothers and sisters can develop the student much faster than training alone. Mindfulness of these principles within the forms brings the form alive and into its true conception. To study, comprehend, and articulate the principles is regarded as the scholarly side of the arts and is a step on the path to full attainment of the system. In order to fully understand Seven Star Mantis, one must have a qualified teacher with a clear systematic formula for giving martial instruction and have studied for many years.

The twelve soft techniques provide an example of taking techniques and applying them in different situations. The terms "soft" or "flexible" imply that the techniques are not strength based. However they still can be extremely powerful, deceptive, and explosive. The terms "soft" and "flexible" like "hard" and "rigid" are similar yet all are different. Praying Mantis Kung Fu is known for its shorthand techniques. These skills must be felt to fully understand; these skills do not exist in words but in the master.

Professionalism

Don't ever do anything as though you were an amateur. Anything you do, do it as a professional to professional standards. We stand on the shoulders of giants.

Make sure that whatever you do in life you're all in. Don't half-way do anything, there'll be no satisfaction in it because there will be no real production you can be proud of. Work your wish boards, your 4 squares, your daily affirmations and write-up your short and long term goals. Decide, commit and succeed. Like the successors before us, our goal is self-mastery.

Develop the frame of mind that whatever you do, you are doing it as a professional and move up to professional standards in it. Never let it be said of you that you lived an amateur life. Professionals see situations and they handle what they see. Never forget that in every situation there's an opportunity.

So learn this as a first lesson about life. The only successful beings in any field, including living itself, are those who have a professional viewpoint and make themselves professionals, and we are professionals. We are what we do; be the change you want to see. We are what we do; always do your best.

With this I would like to say thank you for reading my book, I hope you were able to take something positive away from it. Be mindful of the Three Battles; Mind / Body / Spirit.

Respect and gratitude to all those who helped me with this book.

Train Hard, Train Smart, Finish Healthy and Have Fun!

Sifu Jeffrey Thomas Hughes, 鐵 螳 螂 Iron Mantis Clan

IRON MANTIS MARTIAL ARTS

CONTACT US:

📞 (737) 270-5353

✉ sifuhughes@gmail.com

🌐 www.ironmantismartialarts.com

📷 @sifujeff

Made in the USA
Middletown, DE
22 July 2023